FROM STREET URCHIN TO MAYOR

DENNIS MEREDITH

(Revised & edited by Peter H. Dietrich)

I dedicate this book to my sister, Irene, who was there for me all those years ago when I needed a helping hand, and to all the residents of the Talavera District in Northampton, for putting their trust and faith in me.

To Zhon
from Dennis Meredith.
17/2/25.

CHAPTER ONE

The next stage

If you have read the first volume of my autobiography, you will already know what happened in my life before the journey I was about to undertake, with which this second volume is concerned.

While still working for British Leyland, I felt this job was about to end because of the trouble I was having with my back. The heavy lifting of the large aluminium bellhousings was getting to be too much for me, and every day I'd struggle to lift the heavy load onto the radial drill, a very heavy piece of equipment which I had to use, boring out the hole for the starter-motor fitting.

I had visited the doctor for some treatment, and he referred me to the hospital. I undertook all kinds of exercises to try to cure the pain at the top of my spine. The doctor told me that it could be because I was so tall, and that this problem happened to a lot of tall people, and I understand then that some suffered a similar experience with their backs. When I left British Leyland and the heavy drilling, I never suffered the problem with my back again.

One day in 1972 while sitting at my tea-break, one of my colleagues lent me the Daily Mirror, and leafing through it I noticed an advert from British Timken, a firm in Northampton who were looking for experienced machine operators. Training would be given, and it also mentioned that a new house would be made available by Northampton Development Corporation. I was very interested on reading that advert, and that same day I told my wife about the advert I'd seen and asked for her opinion. She told me it was up to me, and whatever I decided she would support me.

I found the address and telephone number and made an appointment to go for an interview. The person on the phone told me they were doing interviews on a certain date, and so I fixed an appointment in a Central London hotel, although I don't remember the name.

I didn't have a car then, so I went by the underground and arrived for the interview at 10 o'clock. There were several people also waiting to be interviewed, and we were offered coffee and biscuits while we were waiting. When it was my turn to be interviewed, I entered the room and found a well-dressed man sitting behind a desk. I was little bit nervous, but still quite enthusiastic about finding out all about this new life I was considering. He shook my hand and told me that he was from British Timken. He then questioned me about what I was doing at present and asked if I was working in engineering. After answering all his questions, he told me that I would qualify for a job at British Timken.

He went on to ask me about the wages I was earning, and when I told him his face dropped a little. I was earning £50 a week at British Leyland back then, which was paid every Friday. I suppose that made me seem like a millionaire of the working class, because it was well above the average wage at the time. I also suspected that because I was a shop steward and a union activist, he might not offer me a job, because I knew that if you were involved in trade unions in those days a lot of firms wouldn't want to employ you. I had attended a lot of union meetings, and that's where I first got my interest in politics.

The interviewer went on to tell me that they worked a three-shift system, and that I wouldn't earn that kind of money if I went to work at British Timken, but I wasn't really interested in the money at that time. All I was thinking about was a brand-new house and a future for my daughters, Heather and Jennifer. He offered me a job then and said he would put my name forward for a house in Northampton. He took my details and said they'd be in touch with me by letter confirming they had offered me a job. But he also told me there was a waiting list of about three months for a house. I shook his hand and thanked him, then went straight home to tell Rona the good news about the job and that we'd be moving to Northampton in the near future. Rona was very pleased, and she said again that she would support me whatever I did in the future.

The following day I returned to work at British Leyland, where I had a friend, Les Greenhead, who worked on the automatics with me. We had quite a good rapport, and during our lunchbreaks we'd sit in the canteen and tell each other different stories. I kept in touch with him after I left British Leyland, and we'd take turns talking to each other on the phone.

He was a member of the Labour Party and told me all about them and what they stood for. We had a lot of discussions about the Labour Party and the Labour movement in general, and I quickly became interested in socialism. He tried to convince me to join the Labour Party on several occasions, while I grew interested in a different view of politics. I was in my late 20s when I attended several left-wing meetings. I then joined the Workers Revolutionary Party and would stand outside Hammersmith Underground Station selling the local paper, while trying to persuade people to come to our meetings. I also became interested in the trade unions at the same time and was involved in the trade union movement at British Leyland. But I didn't join the Labour Party until I moved to Northampton.

This was a very exciting time for myself and Rona, as we arranged to bring my daughter Jennifer back into our family. When I lived in Basingstoke, I'd been obliged to place Jennifer in a foster home as I had to return to fulltime work and the Social Services weren't able to help me care for her. Now I arranged with Hampshire Social Services for Jennifer to come and live with us in London. She was living in Camberley, in Surrey, with a foster mother, Mrs. Hutton. She was a very kind and loving person and had always taken great care of Jennifer. We arranged for Rona to go to Camberley to fetch her, as I was working fulltime and couldn't get the time off.

We fixed a date and time with Mrs Hutton to pick up Jennifer, and Rona took a coach to Camberley. She told me later that Mrs. Hutton had seemed a little upset to see Jennifer go, but she knew it was the best thing for her to return to live with her parents. I got home at around 6 o'clock that evening, and it was an emotional and moving reunion for all of us.

Jennifer was overjoyed to be living with us, and we had some great times together in London. We visited the local park a great deal together and had many excursions around London on my days off work. She quickly settled into our family, and then one day Rona told me she was pregnant. I was really excited about what was going to happen, although it meant that Rona would eventually have to give up her job at the hospital. My second daughter, Heather, was born in Northwick Park Hospital, and so I found myself with a complete family: myself, Rona, and my two daughters, Jennifer and Heather.

Rona began working in Harrow as a nurse at the geriatric hospital, looking after elderly people, which helped us with our financial situation. One story she told me and that has stayed in my mind concerned an elderly lady who was very poorly, and who asked the nurses if they would get her some jellied eels. Because of her poor state of health, someone would have to feed her with the jellied eels, but most of the nurses couldn't bring them themselves to do it because they didn't like jellied eels. So, Rona volunteered, and she told me that the old lady really enjoyed those jellied eels. She passed away the following day, and Rona was so happy that she'd been able to give a little pleasure to this elderly lady in her final hours.

The time seemed to drag while waiting for the new job and house in Northampton, but then I received a letter from British Timken telling me they had arranged a visit to their factory and to look at the new houses in Northampton, and both Rona and I were excited by the prospect. They had arranged a coach trip for us from Victoria Coach Station, and we arrived at 9am and took the coach to Northampton. Our first impressions of Northampton were quite different from what we'd expected. I'm not sure what we were expecting exactly, but it looked to be very outdated when compared with London.

Back then, Northampton was quite different to how it is at present, but all we could think about at that time was the house we would be offered. So, we had a tour of the factory, and then went to look at the houses. We visited two new estates, one at Thorplands and the other at Lumbertubs. I had no idea at that time that one day I would be representing both those estates with the Borough and the County Council.

We opted for the Lumbertubs estate, as we weren't too keen about the oil central heating in the houses on the Thorplands estate. We were both very excited on visiting the house, which was the completed show-house. The other houses weren't quite ready, and they explained that it would be about five weeks before we could move into the house and then begin the job at British Timken.

Shortly before we moved, I'd become quite an enthusiast of greyhound racing. My brothers were also into greyhound racing, and we used to visit a farm where the greyhounds stayed before going on to the racetracks. On some of those visits we talked with a man who bred greyhounds for racing, and one time he asked me if I'd be interested in buying one. If so, I could pick one from a new litter of six. I was very interested, because at that time I loved all those dogs, and I'd sometimes take some of them for walks across the fields.

I bought a dog for £25, and that was my first venture into greyhound racing. I grew excited at the prospect of watching my dog run at Wembley Stadium. The person who owned the farm was Mrs. Finlay, and she agreed to look after my dog until it got older. I used to go over there every week then and take it out for a walk, and so it quickly got to know me. I named it **CINDY**, but this wasn't its track name. When it was a year old, I had to register it, and **CINDY** became officially **JENNY'S DELIGHT**, named after my daughter, of course.

Dennis with his greyhound

I took my dog to be schooled by a person named Paddy Mulligan, who was very experienced in training greyhounds to run as he owned his own greyhound track. After a time, he told me that Cindy was ready to race, and that she was a good dog as she'd achieved very fast times running around his track. In the meantime, I had to make an appointment for the next day with one of the trainers at Wembley. I had to keep the dog in our flat overnight, but as greyhounds aren't house-trained, I had to sit with her on the landing all night, because every time I left her, she'd start barking.

I went to Wembley and met a trainer named Mr Pickering, who took the dog and said he'd get her ready for a trial. The dogs had to achieve a certain time to qualify for racing at Wembley. My dog did qualify, and I was looking forward to her first race. I was notified then that my dog, JENNY'S DELIGHT, would run in the first race on the card. She ran a good race but finished last. I knew at that time that I was moving soon to Northampton, and so I asked my brothers to take over the dog for me. I never learned after that what happened to my dog, as they never told me. But shortly after that I was on my way to Northampton.

CHAPTER TWO

Preparing to move

While waiting to move and to begin working at British Timken, we also had to wait for the Northampton Development Corporation to let us know when the house would be ready for occupation and for us to move in. In the meantime, the pain in my spine seemed to be getting worse and I worried that I wouldn't be fit enough to move to Northampton, although I was more than determined that I would do so.

We eventually got the much-awaited letter and set off to Northampton by train to pick up the keys of the house. We arrived at Northampton Station and took a taxi to the offices of the Northampton Development Corporation, where we were met by the housing officer. He was very pleased to see us, and we had to sign a few papers. Our new address was at 23, Bitten Court, in the Lumbertubs district, and he explained that the rent would be £6.50 per week. I looked at Rona, and we were both a little shocked at facing what seemed to be a high rent for us to pay for a council house. At the same time, I was thinking about the wages I would be earning, which was only £17 per week. But we brushed our worries aside, because we were really thrilled at the prospect of living in a brand-new house.

We made our way to the Derngate bus station and decided to get something to eat at The Lamplighter pub next door to it. After our meal we caught a bus to the Lumbertubs Estate, although it only stopped at Arbours Road. The dual carriageway which runs along the top of the estate was still in the early stages of being developed, and we had to cross the muddy A43 road to reach the Lumbertubs Estate. We eventually found the house, and our shoes were pretty muddy by then, but we weren't too worried about that. We were really excited when opening the door of our new house for the first time and going inside.

Bitten Court – Lumbertubs Estate

We could smell the newness of the house right away, with shiny black tiles in the hallway and the kitchen, and a large front room downstairs. The kitchen looked superb, with an adjoining dining room, while upstairs there were three bedrooms and the bathroom. We looked all around the house, and looking out from it we could see quite a distance and where the new LINGS ESTATE was still being built. We were one of only three tenants on our estate in 1972.

We decided after an hour or so that we should go to the British Timken factory and let them know that we now had the house, and I'd be able to start working for them after a week's holiday. Meanwhile I would have to return to London and let my family know that we were moving to Northampton, where we had a brand-new house and a new job.

Back in London, we went to see my mother and Roy and gave them our news. She wasn't too pleased to hear that we were moving out of London, saying that my brothers and sisters might think that I didn't care about them anymore. I explained to her then about the problems with my back, and how I couldn't carry on with the heavy work I was doing at British Leyland. She then wished me the best of luck and hoped that my future would be good.

And so we began making definite plans for moving to Northampton. Jennifer was six years old at the time, and so she understood about us moving and was very pleased at the idea of living in a new house. Heather, my other daughter, was only six months old and so didn't know about the move. But then it was Rona who appeared to be getting stressed about it. I reassured her as best I could that everything would be all right, and I went ahead with all the arrangements. We hired a self-drive van, and the plan was that I would drive to Northampton with our belongings, and then drive it back to Harrow. We would all then take the train to Northampton. It was going to be a long journey for me, but I was thrilled at the prospect of starting a new life in Northampton.

I have always loved London and had some good times and a good life there. I am still a true Londoner at heart. Everyone in Northampton says they can tell I come from London, and I still think about my place of birth and my upbringing. But I have been in Northampton now for over 50 years, and so I think I can class myself as being something of a Northamptonian.

I returned to work after a few days off and handed in my notice. I was sorry to leave British Leyland, where I'd made lots of friends. One of my colleagues, John Tierney, with whom I used to play darts at the local pub, was godfather to my daughter Heather. Another was Vernon Wilson, from whom I used to borrow money when I was short for my dinner. He was a very smart single man and something of a gentleman, dabbling in shares at the stock exchange, where he did quite well. He had a lot of shares in Tesco. He lived alone and told a lot of stories about his family who lived in Norfolk.

My best friend, Les Greenhead, was really upset about me leaving. He wished me all the best, and as I explained in my first volume, he phoned me regularly in Northampton for quite some time after I left. He was a great influence on my political life.

When I told the union bosses about my moving, they wished me good luck. They were sorry to see me go after working so hard to improve the workers' rights at British Leyland. But personally speaking, I wasn't sorry to be going as my back was still causing me some problems, and I was often in pain when lifting the heavy bell housings. I must have drilled thousands of them during my time at that job.

I sometimes look at the old Routemaster buses at exhibitions in Northampton, and I think to myself that I made the parts for the clutches in them. They were very good buses. The British Leyland factory at Southall is now closed, and I understand that there are now flats and houses on the site. It was a massive site, and when I worked there, they employed up to five thousand people. I was sorry to hear that the site had closed.

I did get a pension from British Leyland, which amounted to £26.50 in total, but I'd completely forgotten about it when I retired at the age of 65. I received a letter from the insurance company with a document I had to sign for the amounts due to me. I was amazed at how they'd found me, because I hadn't given them any forwarding address. I believe it was through my national insurance number that they tracked me down so as to pay me the money.

When the time came for me to leave the company on the Friday afternoon, I walked out of the factory with the whole workforce banging their spanners and hammers against the side of their machines. This was a long-standing tradition when anyone left the company.

CHAPTER THREE

The day finally comes

My mother and Roy came to help us load the van we'd hired, although we didn't have a great deal to move. It was mostly clothes, plus our three-piece suite, our bed, and those of the children. The heaviest thing we had to carry was the old gas stove-cooker, which we had permission from the landlord to take. Roy and myself carried it out to the van, and I wondered then how I was going to carry it into the new house all alone. I knew that Rona couldn't help, as it would have been far too heavy for her. Once everything was packed, we waved goodbye to my mother and Roy and headed towards the motorway. We set off at about 9 o'clock and it was a sunny day. The journey would take just over an hour.

Rona had prepared a flask of coffee and some sandwiches for when we arrived in Northampton, and we pulled-up outside our new home at around 10.30. We were all excited, and especially Jennifer, who rushed about all over the house exploring. Rona took her to her bedroom, and she was enchanted and delighted with it. Then she wanted to help us unload the van. We got all our things into the house, except the heavy gas-stove.

There were only about three or four families in the court when we moved in, and after a short break for the coffee and sandwiches, we had to solve the problem of getting the gas-stove into the house. I saw a builder working on new paving slabs on the opposite side of the road, and so I went over and asked him if he would help me to carry in the gas-stove. He smiled and said he would, and so we carried the gas-stove into the house between us. I thanked him and he wished us all the luck in the world. I saw him again on several occasions, and I soon found out that he too had come to Northampton from London. We got to chatting with each at the local pub and we become quite friendly.

Outside, everything still looked brand-new, and especially all the houses with their newly painted windows and doors, with one of their most outstanding features being the black tiles on the front walls. But after a few hours spent arranging our things in the house, it was time for me to set off back to London to return the van on the following day. Rona come to see me off, and all the way I couldn't stop thinking about our new house and the prospect of starting a new job, wondering how it would all work out.

Having returned the van, I went back to Northampton by train, and as we approached the town, I looked out at the different outskirts we passed through and noticed how they appeared rather rundown, and I wondered then what I had let myself in for. Reaching Northampton, I took a bus home, and when I arrived at the house Rona was really pleased to see me, as was Jennifer. I told them both about my trip with the van to London and my return by train.

We decided to take a few days to get the house sorted out, and that evening I thought I'd go out and try to find a local pub. This turned out to be an experience I would never forget. I've always liked going to a pub for a couple of drinks, and so I set off to find a pub near to where we lived. I crossed the new road, the A43, which was still being built, and I quickly found my shoes full of mud, and soon had mud up to the tops of my knees! When I'd crossed the road, I saw a man walking his dog and I asked him for directions. He pointed me towards the nearest pub called The Lumbertubs. The estate was named after the farm it had been built on. The pub was on the corner of Kettering Road, and I soon managed to find it, but going in I was truly surprised. It wasn't as it is today but consisted of just one small room furnished with old wooden tables, and I was the only customer. I ordered a drink and then sat there wondering again about what I'd let myself in for.

I stayed about an hour, and when I'd finished my drinks, I decided to try to find a better way to get back home. By the time I arrived home I was feeling very depressed and was already missing London. The first thing I said to Rona was how sorry I was for what I'd done by bringing her to Northampton, but she reassured me that everything would turn out to be all right. She'd already been working hard on arranging the house to make it more comfortable, and I must admit that she quickly made it a very pleasant home for me and my family.

CHAPTER FOUR

Working at Timken

After a week spent settling into the new house and exploring the surrounding areas around our new home, the time came for me to start work at Timken, which would eventually turn out to be a nightmare. On my first day, which began at 8am, I had to report to the personnel department for a medical examination with a nurse in the first-aid department. After the medical the nurse told me I was fit to work there, with the only problem being that I was colour-blind, which I already knew about.

The Timken factory at Northampton

After I'd filled in all the forms I was taken to a special classroom for a week's training, to learn and understand the measuring processes while using the automatic machines which made the roller bearings. I started to panic a little because of my dyslexia, afraid I wouldn't be able to read and understand the micrometre and the measurements for the roller bearings.

My first day was spent learning all about what the bearings were and what they were used for. We were shown pictures of certain vehicles and how the bearings in them worked. We were then shown the actual bearings we'd be making on the automatic machines, and how to load the machines with steel tubes. These were very heavy and about 3 metres in length, and the machines held six of them. There was a crane with a hook to lift the bar up into the machine.

This went on for most of the day, and when we finished at 3 o'clock I was surprised to find how long it took me to get from the factory in Duston to Lumbertubs, where I now lived, and I had to take two buses to reach my home. Before I left, I asked the person in charge of the course what sort of wages I'd be earning, and he replied I'd get the early-shift rate during that week's course. At that time, I wasn't too concerned as I believed I'd be earning pretty good money.

The course lasted for the whole week, and on the last day I was told I had passed the test. That meant I would be allowed to start work on the machines and was taken to meet the foreman and the machine setter. They told me my starting shift would be from 2 pm - 10 pm, and I could start work on the following Monday afternoon.

I turned up for work on time and was put straight to work on the heavy automatic machines. I was given instructions and shown how to operate them, and after two days of learning I was told by the machine setter that I would be expected to produce a certain amount of roller bearings on each shift. He then said that for the first week I shouldn't worry about counting the number of bearings I produced, because they wouldn't be counted until I was fully familiarised with the machines.

I quicky adapted to the pattern of the three-shift system, although I could never get used to the night shift, and just six weeks after starting this job I was already feeling very tired and disenchanted with it. I disliked the smell when I walked into the factory and along the alley to my machine, and the constant smell of oil always made me feel sick. I forced myself to stick it out for another six weeks, but the strain of working there seemed to get worse because of the fact that I'd come from London.

One of the machines at Timken

The Northampton residents appeared to be more than resentful of people from other towns coming to Northampton and being given new houses right away, whereas they had difficulties getting one even when they'd been on the Council's waiting list for some time. This meant that people from London, like me and my family, were given a house through the development corporation before any local people qualified for one.

I soon discovered that most of the people working at Timken were from Northampton and the surrounding areas, and I found it very difficult to make any friends with my co-workers. As soon as they found out that I was a Londoner, no-one seemed to want to talk with me apart from the machine setter.

This made me feel even more isolated, as well as making the job less interesting, and at that point I started wishing I could go back to London. I was missing my family and my hometown.

On one occasion while sitting in a café in Northampton Town Centre having a quiet cup of tea, I overheard three men on the next table talking loudly. Their conversation was along the lines that there was now a lot of crime on the new housing developments, and it was all down to the Londoners who had moved in. When I heard that I felt really horrified, and it showed me just how big was the resentment the residents held against the people like me who had come from London. I am glad this doesn't happen today, although the same resentment is now directed at foreign immigrants coming into Britain.

At that time, I felt at my lowest ebb once again. The depression I've suffered from for most of my life was growing steadily worse, and I really did consider moving back to London. But then I began slowly to make a few new friends among the people I worked with, although again they were mostly from London, like me, and in time most of them went back to London because they couldn't adjust to the way of life in Northampton.

One day I was in the canteen during my lunchbreak when a man seated at the same table started talking with me, and I found I got on quite well with him. His job was to collect all the waste materials from the machines and transport it to a place where it would be collected three times a week. He came and sat with me a few more times and we'd chat together, but then after one occasion when returning to my machine, one of the other workers came over to me and told me not to talk to this man anymore, as no-one in the factory ever talked to him. I asked him why, and he told me that this man had been prosecuted for some abnormal acts with an animal! I never tried to find out more or elaborate on any details, so I'll leave it to the reader to make their own conclusions.

Much later, when I was a Councillor, I was door-knocking one day and a lady invited me in for a chat. She introduced me to her husband and told me that he'd worked at Timken for forty years. But now he sat beside an oxygen bottle to help him breathe, and he explained that it was due to the long years he'd spent working at Timken in such a smoky environment. But he also said that he'd loved working there. I felt sorry for him, while thinking how lucky I'd been in not working too long in that same employment. I might well have ended up as he had if I had stayed longer at that factory.

When I was working on the nightshift, I had to leave my house at 7-30pm to catch what was the last bus of the evening from Lumbertubs. I then had to wait in the bus station for another bus that left at 9-30pm to take me to the factory for my shift, which started at 10-30pm. I had to do this for the five days of the nightshift, and it was awful, especially having to wait in the bus station for over an hour each time for my next bus.

After working at Timken for a while I found the wages were quite low, and I was struggling to live comfortably with everyday expenses while paying the rent and other bills. With the three-shift system, I would receive £17 per week on the early-morning shift, £25 per week for the afternoon shift, and £31 per week for the night shift. That was after tax and national insurance had been taken, and as you can see, it really wasn't a lot of money with which to look after my family and manage my finances. A lot of the Londoners who'd moved to Northampton to work at Timken at the same time had already returned to London, and that set me thinking again that perhaps I should do the same.

I had kept a keen interest in the Trade Unions from when working with them in London, but I couldn't find any activity going on by the Amalgamated Engineering Union, which was the union operating at Timken. I decided then to go and talk with the union convener of the factory. When I found him, I told him that I didn't think the wages paid were in line with the job I was doing, and he seemed rather surprised that I questioned him about this. He explained that Timken had a system of calculating their wage-scale with the input and support of the Trade Unions. I could hardly believe what I was hearing from him and told him that the wages were so low that a lot of people were struggling to live, me included.

A few weeks later as I began the nightshift again, I was really struggling. I was at an all-time low and my depression was getting worse again. During the nightshift I was operating the machines as usual, but by this time I'd been obliged to wear a protective hat, as the oil from the machines sprayed out onto my head and so covered my hair with oil.

Rona would make me sandwiches for my break on the nightshift, and I always left them on top of my locker, which was opposite my machine. One night I needed to use the toilets just before my break, and when I came back to pick up my sandwiches they weren't there! Someone had obviously taken them, and that proved to be the last straw for me. I couldn't take any more of this job, and so I simply walked out of the factory. There were no buses at that time of night, and so I had to walk all the way from Duston to my home in Lumbertubs.

And that was my final job in engineering. When I got home, Rona asked me what I was doing there as I should have been working, and so I explained to her how I couldn't cope with the hostile atmosphere and unhealthy environment of that place, and I'd had to get out before it drove me mad.

The Timken factory in Northampton was closed in April of 2021, and it is now a new housing estate.

Finding myself suddenly unemployed and having my family to support, I had to begin planning immediately what I was going to do. I went for an interview for a driving job in Kingsthorpe Hollow, delivering sausages and pies, but when the man told me what the wages would be I couldn't believe it. They were even lower than the Timken wages had been.

I began to wonder again if it wouldn't be better now for me to go back to London, but I decided to carry on for a while longer and try to find a suitable job I could be happy with in Northampton. The following day I met a man named Leo Joseph who lived in a four-bedroomed house in the court next to mine. His place of birth was Pakistan, and he was married to an English lady. He told me he worked as caretaker at Lumbertubs Lower School, and I explained to him how I was now unemployed and was looking for a new job. He suggested then that I apply to become a caretaker of a school, as there were lots of new schools being built, all of which would need a caretaker.

This struck me as being a good idea, as well as something completely different for me. When I first moved to Northampton the local paper, The Chronicle and Echo, was filled with job offers, and so now I carefully looked through all the job-vacancies pages. I spotted an advertisement looking for a caretaker at Kingsthorpe Upper School, which was a brand-new school still being built. I sent off for an application form, and soon received a letter back inviting me to go for an interview.

I went through the interview process with the supervisor of school caretakers, a Mr. Norman Wright, who would become well known to me later. He was a very smart man, well-dressed and well-mannered. Unfortunately, I didn't get that particular job, but two days later Mr. Wright phoned me to tell me that there was a new school being built on the Ling's Estate, and I could go there for an interview. I was really pleased at the prospect, and I thought I was in with a good chance of getting that job.

I spoke to Rona and told her about the new interview, and she agreed it was good idea. Mr. Wright told me that the wages were reasonable, and that it could be a job for life. The interview date was set, and I received a letter to confirm this. I told my new friend, Leo Joseph, that I was going for an interview for the position of caretaker at Lings Lower School, and he visited me at home and explained all about the job and what I should say during the interview. I felt greatly reassured by his comments and his well-timed advice.

CHAPTER FIVE

My new life at Lings Lower School

I attended the interview, but I wasn't feeling too nervous about it as I knew from my prior interview that I should try to present a more positive impression. I was called into an office at the Education Department at Cliftonville, where I was introduced to the headteacher, a Mrs. Keightley. On first impressions she looked to be a warm person, very neat and smartly dressed. I didn't know what headteachers looked like overall, but I presumed her to be a typical female headteacher. Mr. Wright was sitting beside her, and after he introduced me to Mrs. Keightley we shook hands, and she asked me to sit.

She began by asking me to tell her about myself, and so I explained about having moved recently from London with my young family. I also told her that I was no longer happy working in the engineering sector, and that I was looking for a change of direction. The interview appeared to go well, and I think I made quite a good impression. At the end of the interview, Mr. Wright asked me to wait in the next room. I realised that I was the only applicant for the position, and I felt confident that I'd be offered the job.

When I was called back into the office, Mrs. Keightley told me that she'd pleased to offer me the post of caretaker, and I felt completely overjoyed. Mr. Wright then explained that the school hadn't been completed yet, but I could start straight away as caretaker, and that I could also do some basic training at Weston Favell School. That idea pleased me, as there were a few things that I would have to learn before I could start the job.

I had to undergo an obligatory medical examination including an x-ray at the Northampton Hospital Chest Clinic, and I understood that this was for the superannuation that became obligatory after working for the Education Department for one year. I had to wait for the result of the x-ray before I could start work. I received a letter from the hospital shortly after telling me that I had to return for a second x-ray, and I started worrying that there was perhaps something wrong with me. But when I returned to the x-ray department, they explained that the first x-ray wasn't very clear and so they needed to do another one. I was more than relieved at that news, and after a week or so I received the all-clear from the hospital and so could begin work at Weston Favell School.

I turned up at the school on a Monday morning to find Mr. Wright, the superintendent of caretakers, already there, and he introduced me to a man called Peter Brewer, who I understand was an ex-goalkeeper from the local Cobblers football team. I was then taken to a classroom by one of the assistant caretakers, and he started showing me how to use a scrubbing machine on the floor. But while he was cleaning the floor with the machine he slipped and fell over, hitting his head quite hard. There was very soon a lot of blood everywhere, and I wondered what I should do. On my very first day in this job the caretaker had suffered a serious accident.

I rushed back to Peter Brewer's office and told him what had happened, and he called for an ambulance to take the caretaker to hospital, as he was still losing quite a lot of blood. I was then left on my own to mop-up all the blood, which seemed to be everywhere. I learnt a good lesson from that accident, one I would never forget.

I remained at that school for four weeks and I was placed on the minimum wage scale. I had to visit the Cliftonville Education Office to collect my wages, which was still paid weekly in cash at that time. When I collected my first wages and saw how much I received, I told Mr. Wright that it wasn't a lot of money for me to live on and look after my family. He told me not to worry, as when I began work at the new school I'd be working on a bonus scheme, and so I accepted that. The new school was almost ready for me to start working there.

The new housing estates were rapidly taking shape now, and many more houses were almost ready to be occupied. The headteacher of Lings Primary School came to see me then at Weston Favell School and told me that they would soon be opening two classes at her school, and then asked if I would like to go and prepare the classes to be ready for the children to attend. I was quite happy at that idea, because I really wanted to be working permanently in my own school.

I went to look at the two classrooms in question. On one side were the boys' and the girls' toilets, and I saw at once that the classrooms in question had been empty for quite some time and needed a thorough cleaning. I set to work on them straight away, as I'd learnt to use the cleaning machines at Weston Favell School, and how to use the cleaning chemicals. Mr. Wright came to the school, and together we ordered a lot of cleaning supplies from the County Suppliers so that I could carry out the cleaning procedures. Once they were delivered, it didn't take me very long to clean and sort out the two classrooms, and to get the toilets up and running. My headteacher came to inspect the classrooms when I'd finished, and she thanked me and said how nice everything looked now. I felt very pleased with myself.

On the following Monday morning the children started to arrive. To begin with there were only about ten, and so they only used one of the classrooms I'd prepared. At the same time, I was travelling between the Lumbertubs School and my own school, Lings Lower School, taking in deliveries. The builders informed us that we could now use part of the school and all the supplies I was storing in the new part of the school. This was about five weeks before Christmas, and Mrs Keightley gave me the date on which she would bring the children to the part of the school that was now ready. There were about twelve of them, and they were really excited about this new adventure of moving into a brand-new school.

All this was happening just four months after my moving to Northampton, and what a pleasant change it was for me and my family. I knew that I would have a problem with my dyslexia, and I did wonder how I was going to write clearly all the things I would have to as a caretaker. But I needn't have worried, as I decided with Rona that she would do all the writing I had to do. I never mentioned to anyone that I was dyslexic, although I suspect that many of the teaches did know about it. And again, in all the years I worked at the school I never told anyone about my depression, nor how much it affected my life. I kept all of that very much to myself.

The day finally arrived when we could move into the whole of the school and its lovely new building, with carpets everywhere and a very bright atmosphere. It was 2 o'clock in the afternoon when we took the children from Lumbertubs School to their new school, and the sheer excitement coming from them was overwhelming. They started singing in a lovely London accent, as most of them had come from London, just as I had with my family.

I was the first to reach the school, and I had a key to open the front door. Mrs. Keightley told me that she'd chosen to work at this school because it was all open plan, with no separate or individual classrooms. This was a new concept in education, and they were trying it out here. Mrs. Keightley had been appointed as headteacher due to her long teaching experience and her knowledge of open-plan schools, although I could see no real difference. To me, it was just a normal school, although it did strike me as strange that all the classrooms were open, and I did wonder how they would teach the children in this environment. Eventually though it all had to change, because the children couldn't be taught properly in an open-plan school, and they had to section off some of the areas to keep down the noise of the adjacent classrooms. But at least they gave it a try.

Dennis in his caretaker role

On the lead up to Christmas, Mrs Keightley decided that we should have a carol concert for the children and their parents, although we still didn't have a great number of pupils at this time. But she'd decided that we would sing carols, and she asked me to take part in the service. Carol sheets were printed, and Mrs. Keightley asked me to stand at the entrance and hand them out to the parents as they came in. Although there weren't many children to take part the parents joined in, and it was a very joyous occasion for everyone. It was also the first time as a caretaker that I'd done anything like this, and I also enjoyed it a lot.

Many of the teachers also worked throughout the Christmas holiday, unpacking books and receiving deliveries of furniture and many other things needed for the classrooms, as they wanted the school to be ready for after the holidays. The school had opened completely by this time, and so there was a lot of work to be done.

Dennis, Rona & children

At the same time my own two children, Jennifer and Heather, were growing up fast, and I was very proud and fond of them. But on one occasion when all the children on the estate were still young, Heather went missing after she'd been playing outside with the others. Rona couldn't find her anywhere, and after looking for two hours we finally decided to notify the police. I was worried that something dreadful might have happened to her, but then she suddenly came walking into our courtyard as if nothing had happened. I asked her where she'd been, and she told me she'd found a new friend and had been playing in her back garden. I can't tell you how relieved I was, but I had to explain to her that she should never go away from our house without first informing us where she was going. She was a very sensible child, and so I'm glad to say this didn't happen again.

I was very busy now constantly unpacking all kinds of teaching aids that were delivered each day. I had been to the school before it opened to take in the desks and chairs for the classrooms, and I also had to unpack the other larger tables and chairs, but I felt good doing all this, and I knew that I was going to enjoy being the caretaker of this school.

I found it puzzling to find that the school was also completely open on the outside, and so anyone from the estate had easy access to the school. This would soon prove to be a problem, as a lot of vandalism started happening to the outside of the building. And then one morning on arriving at the school I discovered that every single window in the school had been smashed, in all around 250 windows! I was horrified when I saw the mess made by all the broken glass and I immediately telephoned the headteacher.

When she arrived, she asked me to help telephone to all the parents to let them know that the school wouldn't be open that day, and it was quite a mammoth task informing them all. Fortunately, the building department agreed to cover the cost of the replacement windows, but the school would have to remain closed for a while.

I contacted the County Council Education Department, who in turn contacted the contractor who agreed to replace all the windows with reinforced glass for future protection. In the meantime, all the windows had to be boarded up, as the reinforced glass had to be ordered and then fitted. Once the windows were boarded up, which took two days, the children were allowed back into school. It was very strange and almost spooky then, as the lights had to be switched on all day and so the children had their lessons in the semi-darkness, while I found hundreds of glass fragments on the carpets each day which I had to collect and dispose of. The glaziers eventually turned up to install the new windows, and the school had to be closed again for the day while they did this.

I must add that during this incident the teachers were understanding and excellent, and they all helped to get the school back up and running again. It was difficult for everyone to believe that this could have happened to a brand-new school, in which every single one of windows had been broken.

I reported the matter to the local police, who began making enquiries, and they quickly found the culprits: two 10-year-old boys! They'd walked around the school with hammers and smashed all the windows, even the very large windows above the hall for which they'd climbed onto the roof to gain access to them. I was later told by the police that the two boys had been sternly reprimanded and cautioned, but they couldn't be prosecuted as they were under-aged at the time.

During the early weeks of the school the headteacher decided to organise a mammoth Carnival, which would take place in the top playground. As caretaker, I wasn't really looking forward to such an event, as I knew it would mean a lot of extra work for me. It took around three months of preparation to organise it all, and I can still remember the name of the girl who was going to be Carnival Queen for the day: Amanda Spence. She was excited, as were all the other children, and a great many costumes had to be made for them and all the other events planned and organised.

The big day finally arrived, and all the children were dressed up in their costumes, with every single one in their unique costume. The parents were all cheerfully seated around the playground, and there were even two donkeys to pull the cart with the Carnival Queen and her attendants seated upon it, and there were a lot of other floats in the procession around the playground. It was a huge success, and the parents thoroughly enjoyed the day, as did the Carnival Queen, Amanda. I sometimes wonder where she is and what she's doing now.

When it was over and the children had gone home with their parents, I started cleaning-up the mobile classrooms which had been left on-site in the playground. As I was cleaning one of them, a young woman appeared on the steps and asked me what I was doing. I explained to her that I was cleaning-up after the Carnival, and then I noticed that she had a razorblade in her hand. Without warning she then slashed her wrist right there in front of me!

There was blood gushing everywhere, and I was quickly covered with blood myself. I grabbed her wrist and held it tightly to try to stop the bleeding, and then I led her down to the school while holding and pressurising her wrist as best I could. There was a vivid trail of blood left everywhere we passed. Thankfully, the headteacher was still in her office, and she fetched the first-aid kit and wrapped the wound to stem the bleeding before calling for an ambulance. When it arrived, the first reaction of the crew was to tell us that they knew this person very well, and that she was quite a regular visitor at the hospital.

After a short time, the vandalism at the school was becoming more and more frequent and out of control. It was also costing the County Council a great deal of money for the repairs which needed doing rapidly for the school's safety. It got to a point where almost every day something else had been damaged on the outside of the school, and this was also taking me away from all my other regular tasks as caretaker. I suggested then to the headteacher that the County Council should erect a metal Palisade fencing around the whole school to keep the vandals out during the night.

She wrote then to a Mr. Graham Smith at the Architects' Department, who was the liaison officer with the County Council Building Control, and he agreed that the cost of the constant repairs was getting out of hand. He asked me to record just how much vandalism we had suffered over the past twelve months and what had taken place, which I did, and it was a pretty long list indeed.

On one occasion when I was sitting in the staffroom, I heard a scream from outside and I rushed out to see what had happened. I found a young woman sobbing hysterically. When I managed to calm her down a little, she told me that a man had grabbed her and tried to pull her into the hedge surrounding the school, where he'd tried to rape her. She'd managed to break free and had run into the school.

I immediately called the police and told them about the incident, and two policewomen came to talk with the woman. I made her some coffee while we were waiting for the police, and she did calm down a little. But after this terrible incident it was of vital importance to get a secure fence erected around the school grounds.

Three months later we received the good news that a fence was to be erected around the school perimeter, and we all breathed a sigh of relief. I knew that this would keep the school safe and secure, and that the idea of schools being open and accessible to the public with no protection at all had been a very unwise idea. A high and solid metal fence was soon in place around the whole school grounds, and it did put a stop to the vandalism while making my job a whole lot easier.

At this time most wages had been regularly increasing along the national inflation figures, and I was receiving quite a decent wage. But then the County Council decided that they were going to restructure the wages of caretakers under their charge, and I knew at once that this would be bad news for me. The position of caretaker would be renamed as Cleaner-in-charge in all the Lower Schools, and that would halt the bonus system we caretakers were then working under. A terrible decision for me at the time, although the County Council were notorious for doing this type of thing. But my headteacher insisted that I was still a caretaker, and I would not be classed as a Cleaner-in-charge.

This one the first of many tribulations I would have with the County Council over the years, as they were always looking for ways of preventing their employees from earning too much money. But I was eventually made a site supervisor, and the then headteacher, Mr. Adams, who was always very good with me, decided to give me a decent wage. In return I had to do all the repairs and some of the gardening, and so I had a lot more responsibility, but I didn't mind and that was how it remained until I retired from my position as caretaker.

Dennis the caretaker opening an event at the school

CHAPTER SIX

Christmas at Lings Lower School

At the end of the term, in the run-up to Christmas, the headteacher came to see me in my office and explained that she'd organised a Carol-singing concert for the children and their parents, but as there weren't enough children to sing she wondered if I'd join-in to help make up the numbers, and also to hand out the Carol sheets. I thought it very thoughtful of her to ask me, and as this would be my first interaction with the children I agreed with pleasure.

Instead of the usual evening carol concert, she invited the parents to attend in the afternoon, and I gave out the carol sheets as they arrived. I recall that at that time there were only about fifteen children, but it all went off well and the children, and myself, received a lovely round of applause.

This would become a special event for every Christmas period, and preparations would begin sometime in October when the children would start practicing their carol singing, which made it sound more polished at the concert.

Mrs. Keightley then thought it would be a good idea for the staff to put on a pantomime for the children, and I was also roped-in for this. I was to be one of the ugly sisters, and then the following year I played the giant in Jack and the Beanstalk. I was told this was because I was naturally so tall.

The children loved the performances, and for me this was the first time I'd done anything like this. My only problem was my dyslexia, which made it more difficult for me to learn my lines for the parts. But I still didn't tell anyone about this and simply made up a lot of my own lines during the performance.

The children enjoyed the plays, and this continued for a few years until some of the staff dropped out or moved on, and that put an end to the staff performing for the children. I remember when I was at school in London that the teachers always put on a pantomime for the children.

After several months of working at the school I found I was still struggling to pay my bills, as my wages weren't that good, and Rona couldn't go out to work because our daughter Heather was still quite young and needed looking after. At one point I completely ran out of money, and I became quite desperate.

I went to see Mrs. Keightley and explained my situation, telling her that I couldn't stay on in that job. She was very sympathetic and informed me that she didn't want me to leave. I had discussed all this with Rona, and I was very serious at that time about moving back to London. Mrs. Keightley then asked me if she could help in any way, and so I explained to her that I couldn't even do any basic shopping for food and other necessities at that time, and so could see no alternative but to return to London.

She asked me not to do that, and then told me that she could help me a little. She asked me to return to my office and wait for her while she went to her home to take some money. I felt terrible, because I did enjoy my job and didn't want to have to leave it now. She returned after about half an hour and handed me £5. I felt ashamed, but I took the money out of desperation, and later I went shopping with Rona and we bought a week's supply of food and other necessities. This was over forty-five years ago, when £5 went a lot further than it would today.

She also asked me if I would be prepared to take on a part-time job, and I told her that I would. She then explained that if I went to her husband's garage on the Wellingborough Road, he would let me work at the petrol pumps during my rest breaks at the school. I was delighted with that idea, and I went to meet her husband who turned out to be a good man who bent over backwards to help me. The extra money I earned at his garage was more than useful, and it did help solve my immediate financial problems.

I then paid a visit to the Social Services and asked if they could help me, and they informed me that they ran a scheme where if wages were lower than a certain figure, they were able to top it up. I also qualified for free milk and vitamin tablets, and that was also a huge help and helped me through the bad patch I was going through financially. It also helped me decide to carry on with my job as caretaker.

In the early days of living on the new estate, there was only one shop close-by where we could buy our groceries, and this was at the bottom end of the estate. In the Lumbertubs shopping complex there was a paper-shop, a small supermarket, and a fish and chip shop. The Development Corporation built the shops and rented them to different people, but we could only get our main groceries in the small supermarket, where the prices were quite high. That's when I decided I must try to earn some extra money somehow.

CHAPTER SEVEN

Weston Favell Shopping Centre

Everyone around us at that time was waiting for the new Weston Favell Shopping Centre to be completed, and a lot of people on the estate were excited at the prospect of having a Tesco Supermarket nearby at which they could shop. The building had been going on for some time, and I once watched as four helicopters passed over our house carrying parts of the roofing to be placed on top of the new building. That was 49 years ago now, and we have just celebrated the 50 years of the Centre being opened.

When it was nearing completion, I was approached by a Mr. Gibson of the Development Corporation who invited me to attend the opening ceremony. It was a grand day, with a great many speeches and activities taking place, and I still remember the first time we shopped at the Tesco supermarket and how it was so much cheaper than at our local shop in Lumbertubs.

The advent of the Weston Favell Centre was a huge life-changing event for the residents of the Lumbertubs and Lings estates, and the pub inside that was named The Swinging Sporran. It was licensed to Young's brewery, a Scottish firm, and the decoration and carpets were all different tartan patterns, with paintings of Scottish landscapes on the walls. They also served a Scottish bitter, which was a good pint of beer much appreciated by the customers. Whenever Rona and I went to shop in the centre we would pop into the pub for a drink, and there was soon quite a large community of regular users which made it easy to meet people and have a chat.

I often met with some of my friends who used the pub regularly, one of whom was an Irishman named Paddy, and we used to drink together quite a lot. I remember on one occasion there being another Irishman in the pub, and Paddy and this other Irishman got into some kind of argument. Paddy called him an Irish bum, and one of my other friends turned to him and asked him if he too wasn't an Irish bum! That really made us all laugh, and the two Irish men quickly made up again.

I can recall that on another occasion, one Christmas Eve, I spent the evening with my friends at the Swinging Sporran, and we had a fabulous time playing records on the jukebox and singing along with the music. Unfortunately, as the Weston Favell Centre became more developed with further shops and cafes, they eventually closed the pub. I always believed this was a great mistake, as a great many people in the community frequented that pub and had made it their local.

I also became quite friendly with the owner of the fish-and-chip shop in the centre, but eventually he sold his licence to another family, who developed it into a Chinese take-away as well as a fish-and-chip shop. Then eventually the paper shop also disappeared when they transformed it into a large supermarket.

Another big event was seeing the Mill Wheel pub being built, which was to become my local. I had some great times there and met a lot of new and good friends. It has long-since closed now, and it was transformed into a Community Hub which is run by a local family. Part of the building is also used as a prayer room. Southfield's Community Centre was also demolished by the Borough Council, against my better judgement. They claimed it was unsafe and that they didn't have the necessary finance to repair it. I thought it was a disaster, and the whole Community Centre is now a play area.

Dennis with the Mayor of Northampton, Councillor Paul Joyce and his Mayoress, Mylissa Joyce, at the 50th anniversary of the Weston Favell Shopping Centre.

Cllr. Joyce was a pupil at Lings Lower School when Dennis was caretaker there; here he is seen holding the first volume of Dennis's autobiography.

CHAPTER EIGHT

Continuing work at Lings Lower School

Continuing with my job as caretaker at the school, I also kept my part-time job at the garage, and then one day the headteacher asked me if I might be interested in becoming a canteen dinner-supervisor, which would also mean extra money, and so I duly applied for that position.

I attended an interview with the head of school meals, and when I walked into her office, she seemed very surprised to see that I was a man who wanted to be a dinner-supervisor looking after children. Back then it was always women who took that job, known as dinner-ladies. I explained to her how I really needed the extra money, which was about £3 per week, but that was a lot of money in those days. I also told her that a lot of the children at my school were sometimes difficult to handle, as they came from London and weren't very disciplined, and that I was also willing to organise various activities for them after dinner.

I got the appointment, and I stayed with it for thirty years. Things were beginning to look up for me at last, and after a while Rona joined me as a cleaner and we worked together for two years. She would bring Heather and Jennifer with her while she did the cleaning. At that time our wages were based on a bonus scheme, and so cleaners earned a good wage. When another cleaner left, Rona and I decided we could clean the whole school between us, and that went on for two years, and so we were quickly coping with our bills again.

Our rent was £6.50 per week, although there was a scheme in which the Education Department would help to pay my rent, and so I only had to pay £1.50 per week, which the Council deducted from my salary. Wages were still paid in cash back then, and I had to go to the Cliftonville office each Friday to collect my wages and to bring back the mail for my school.

I decided to look for more part-time jobs, which I found quite easily. Some of the work I found included several gardening jobs, and then mostly cleaning at the Oven Door, at a local chip shop, at a dentist, and at the Anglia Building Society. The main drawback of this extra work was that I rarely got home before midnight, and I always felt exhausted, although these jobs all helped me to survive as caretaker of Lings Lower school.

I was once having a drink in a local pub when a man next to me asked me how much I was getting paid for one of the extra jobs I was doing. When I told him £5, he said that he wouldn't even get out of bed for that sort of money! I replied that he wouldn't then have that extra money in his pocket, whereas I did on a regular basis. I have always remembered that remark and have always been motivated to work hard and not care about what anyone might say or think about me.

During my employment at the school, I worked under eight different headteachers, each of whom had their own styles and methods of how to run the school. I won't say here which one I considered to be the best out of the eight, although I did have my opinions back then. It wouldn't be fair of me now to say who I thought of as the best, and so I'll keep that to myself. To be fair, they were all good in their own distinct ways, and each of them always treated me with respect.

Mrs. Keightley was the first headteacher I worked for, and I have already related here how kind and helpful she was with me from my beginnings as a caretaker. Mr. Keal drove me mad; although he was a lovely man and a good teacher and the children really liked him, but at the end of each day his classroom was a complete shambles.

The next teacher to take up the headship was a Mr. Adams, and he was followed by a Mrs. Balshaw. She was a lovely person, and I remained friends with her until she passed away. Her husband was the head of the Parks at the Northampton Borough Council, and I was deeply upset when I heard of her death. Sadly, I didn't attend her funeral as nobody notified me, but I did manage to phone her son and offered him my condolences. I will never forget Mrs. Balshaw, who was a kindly and lovely lady.

In the same vein, I will never forget the next headteacher, Mrs. Pitts, with whom again I got on very well. Her husband worked at Goldings Middle School, and I helped to open that school in my spare time. Mr. Pitts was the only teacher from that school who ever spoke with me. I thought at that time he was a lovely man. I knew him for several years.

I was delighted to meet both Mrs. Pitts and Mrs. Davies forty years later when I was Mayor of Northampton. Mrs Davies had been a teacher at the school and was delighted to see me, and we found we had a lot to talk about. I will always remember Mrs Davies as she always told parents not to let young children have number ones on their heads, as it affected their behaviour. I think she may have been right.

Mrs. Jordan was headteacher for one year, and then after her came a Mrs. Marsden. She had been headteacher for about two years when her husband died suddenly of a heart attack, after which she couldn't bring herself to stay on at the school.

I had many conversations with her, and especially when she had to oversee the changes in the Schools System after the County Council decided to close all the middle-schools so as not to have Comprehensive Education. I'd always believed that Comprehensive Education was a better system, and it was distressing to me that they elected to go down another route.

Following on from Mrs. Marsden was a Mrs. Sutcliffe, with whom again I become quite friendly, and Rona and I went out for dinner a few times with her and her husband. She had moved from somewhere in the north to teach in Northampton, and she was always very supportive of me.

To return to Mr. Adams, I found that he was very good with the children, and he would sit and have his dinner with them in the canteen, which always impressed me. He was also good to me, and it was through his intervention that I managed to get wage increases until I was one of the top wage earners among school caretakers. I thank him now for all the help he gave me. All in all, I could thank every headteacher under whom I worked as caretaker, as they all helped me in their own way, and I will be eternally grateful for that.

During my time as a dinner-supervisor at the school, the pupil population increased to around three hundred, and I came to play an important role in helping to look after the children during the lunch breaks. Sometimes It could also be a challenge for me, as quite a few of them lived in one-parent families, and so often had no father-figure to whom they might look up. A lot of the men who came to Northampton when I did had already returned to London.

A few of the children went through some upsetting experiences, and over time they began telling me about their problems and tribulations. I think I possessed a natural understanding for them due to my own traumatic upbringing.

I would often play football with the boys to keep them entertained, and I always found myself in goal at one end of the playground. Some of them would place their coats on the ground to serve as goalposts, and that reminded how we did the same when I was a child playing football in the streets with my friends.

On one occasion, I was approached by a deputation of four girls who asked me why I was always playing football with the boys but never played with any of the girls. This was something I'd never even thought about, and so I asked them what sort of game they would like to play, to which they answered netball. There were no posts in the playground for any such game, and so after the lunch break I called on the headteacher and told her the story. She smiled at this and told me that she'd order two netball posts.

When the posts arrived I placed them in the playground, and when the boys come running out with their football I explained that there would be no football that day, and all their faces dropped at once. Then I told them that we would be playing netball with the girls instead, and that I would play on the girls' team. The boys said that was unfair as I was so tall and so always scored easy goals, but they all soon enjoyed playing this new game, boys and girls together, and I was never accused of only playing with the boys again. I also organised skipping-rope matches, in which I again encouraged the boys to take part with the girls.

During my time as a dinner supervisor, when playing football after dinner in the playground with a group of boys, some of them showed a natural talent and skill that made them stand out. I remember one particular boy as being very talented, and I even sent a letter to the Arsenal Football Club telling them about him and his protentional skill as a professional player, but I never heard back from them.

Then the boys asked me if they could play friendly matches with other schools, which I thought a splendid idea, and so I organised a football match with the children of Abington Vale Lower School. I knew a former teacher at our school, Mrs. Forrester, who now worked there, and so I phoned her to ask if they had a football team and if it would be possible for my team to come and play them. She was also enthusiastic, and so we arranged for me to accompany my team to Abington Vale School for a friendly football match. Well, I believed it would be friendly.

We set off in two cars, with me and a teacher in charge, and the boys were all excited. When we arrived at the school, I asked Mrs. Forrester if she had any string, and when she asked me why I needed string I told her that some of our boys didn't have football boots, and so would have to play in their everyday shoes. As a few of them had no laces in their shoes, they would need string to tie their shoes to keep them on while playing football.

I lectured my boys a little about behaving themselves and to play the best game they could. Then I saw the Abington Vale team running out with their manager, who was going to serve as referee. He was dressed in a proper referee's uniform, and all his team were wearing what looked to be brand-new football kit and shiny football boots, whereas my boys' team wore their everyday shirts with a coloured band crossed over their shoulders. The contrast was starkly obvious.

The game started normally, and I told Mrs. Forester, who was standing next to me, that I hoped her team wouldn't score the first goal. She asked me why, and I told her to wait and see. And when, shortly after, the Abington Vale team scored a goal, all hell seemed to break loose! I was unable to control my boys, who began shouting and swearing, and one boy even punched another boy from the opposing team. When the game ended, Mrs. Forester turned to me and told me not to bring my children to her school ever again, and that, sadly, spelt the end of any football matches with other schools.

Throughout my time as dinner-supervisor the children really came to appreciate and enjoy the games I organised with them, but as I got older, I couldn't always manage to join in the football and netball matches, although I did my best to carry on and to encourage them.

And now, even today some forty years later as I'm writing this memoir, some of the now grown-up children from the school remember me and often approach me to share with me their own memories, and so I think I must have been a good influence upon them. And the present Mayor of Northampton (2024), Paul Joyce, was also a pupil at my school and I can remember looking after him in the playground.

When I first started as caretaker and would help Mrs. Keightley unpack the new goods for the school, she would always refer to me as Mr. Meredith. I asked her once why she didn't call me Dennis, and she replied that that wasn't the custom in schools concerning the caretakers, who were always referred to by their surnames. And this remained so throughout my time at Lings Lower School and any other schools I helped with in their opening stages; I was always known as Mr. Meredith by the staff and pupils alike. I was responsible for helping to open five new schools, and I think this must be a record. But what good times they were for me, truly.

Revisiting Lings school after retiring, with Mayor Stephen Hibbert

CHAPTER NINE

Joining the Church

There was a knock at my door one morning, and when I opened it, I saw a young priest standing there. He introduced himself to me as Father Calnan and told me that he'd just moved into the area. He was living opposite us in Arbour Court, and had discovered that we were a Catholic family, and so wondered if we'd like to attend a service on the following Sunday. It would take place at the house he was renting from the council. I told him that I'd be happy to attend and would bring my family, as we had attended church in London on a regular basis.

Father Calnan

On the Sunday we went over to the priest's house and found just ten people there to celebrate the mass. I quickly became a good friend of Father Calnan, and I questioned him about any plans to build a catholic church on the eastern side of the town. He told me there were plans in the offing, and that he'd let me know when it might be built. About five weeks later, he had to move the Sunday services from his house as the congregation was getting larger, and so he moved them into the Brookside Community Centre. A lot more families were moving into the new estates, and it began to look and feel more like a community on the Lumbertubs Estate.

Houses were filling up with families arriving from London, some of them Catholics, and eventually we had to move our Sunday masses to St Mary's School in Grange Road. The mass took place at 10.30 each Sunday morning, and people began attending from further afield in Northampton. The planners of the Northampton Development Corporation had made quite a few mistakes when planning the estates, one of the worst being the A43 road which split the eastern side of the town into a separate section, and even today it separates the eastern side of the town from the rest of Northampton. But despite this our services were soon very well attended at our new venue, and both my children enjoyed going with us to the mass at St Mary's. They both received their first communion there, and Heather was confirmed there with the Bishop of Northampton officiating. That was the first time I met the bishop.

When plans were eventually made and approved to construct a new catholic church opposite the Weston Favell Shopping Centre, I went with my family to the laying of the foundation stone. There were quite a few people present, including Bishop Grant, the bishop of Northampton. The foundation stone was laid and duly blessed, and the construction work got underway. Six months later the church was completed, and so now we had our own church which really stood out, as it was shaped like a pyramid.

Sacred Heart Church

View of the interior

Dennis as Mayor before the altar

During a service

Dennis and Rona

Dennis and Rona before the entrance

The church is built in a dip, with the parish social facilities and attached presbytery located at the lower level, and the church above, reached by a concrete bridge from the footpath. Behind the altar on the wall of the sanctuary is a striking large painting of the Last Supper by Martin Hughes, a local artist. On the other three walls are further large paintings by Hughes, including the Way of the Cross, some twenty feet high. The benches were made by the local joinery firm of Alan Blenkinsop. The organ console is on the left-hand side, with its pipes located in a projection over the entrance. At each side of the sanctuary are steps leading down to the sacristy, presbytery and parish hall. The church was packed when it opened, and I have attended that church regularly now for fifty-two years.

I then joined the Vincent De Paul Society and quickly became a brother in the organisation. They help a lot of people who are struggling in their daily lives, providing furniture and other basic household needs, and visiting people in hospitals and lonely isolated people who need moral and friendly support. The society is still very active in the community today, and I have often helped raise funds for the organisation. When I was Mayor of Northampton from 2022 - 2023, I raised the amount of £7000 for them, which helped the society continue to help people from all walks of life.

I have also contributed personally from my Councillors' Empowerment salary from the Northampton Town Council, and I am very pleased at how the Society has used such donations to provide Christmas hampers and meals for many elderly people living alone and by organising outings to Wickstead Park, in Kettering, for many deprived children.

I was asked by Mr. Gibson, of the Northampton Development Corporation, if I would organise an event to help bring the community together, as a lot of Londoners were still returning to London when they found it difficult to settle in Northampton. I came up with the idea of staging a community barbecue, and started looking for someone with the necessary experience to help me organise it all. As I had no success, I had to take it upon myself to set-up the barbecue and then cook all the sausages and the other meats.

We decided to hold the event at the Brookside Community Centre, and I arranged for a local band to come and play. I enlisted the help of my wife, Rona, and some of our neighbours who also wanted to help. The Northampton Development Corporation donated £200 for printing leaflets and advertising, which was a great help for the Lumbertubs Residents Association, of which I was chairman. We were well prepared, and quite a few members turned up on the day to help.

I had no idea of the number of people who would turn up for this event, but we had also hired a Punch-and-Judy act to entertain the children who accompanied their parents. I can still remember the Punch-and-Judy puppet-master, who was named Syd Little, although he wasn't related to the famous comic star of the same name. I had hired the same act for my youngest daughter's birthday party when she turned six, and he set up his show in my house, and all the children were really excited as most had never seen a Punch-and-Judy act before.

On the day of the barbecue, we made sure everything was ready with the help of some of the nearby residents. Then we began cooking the burgers and sausages, which filled the air with a delicious aroma and attracted everyone's attention. We had decided to charge a small nominative price for these and so make a little money for the Residents Association.

Soon everything was in place for what was to be our first community event, and people turned up almost at once until we had at least a hundred people milling around and ordering food and drinks from the barbecue stall. We were a little overwhelmed, though pleased with the turnout, while the barbecue was going very well. The children really enjoyed the Punch-and-Judy show, and then everyone enjoyed the band that began playing shortly after, and the whole event went on all through the day until early evening. We were all exhausted but well satisfied by the end of the day, and Mr. Gibson of the Development Corporation congratulated us and thanked everybody for their efforts.

The Northampton Development Corporation was set up by the Labour government to provide houses, jobs and infrastructure for the people of London who chose to move to Northampton.

Some local councillors were on the board of the Development Corporation, and I remember two of them in particular, Councillor Tony Berry and Councillor Tony Woods, both of whom played a very important role in implementing the Development Corporation's plans for the eastern side of the town.

Some fifty years later, a play was produced at the Royal & Derngate Theatre in Northampton, with the title **'60 Miles by Road and Rail'**, and I played an important part in its conception by giving the director a lot of information concerning the activities of the Northampton Development Corporation. I attended a performance of the play before it opened and I found it quite riveting, having been part of the story related when I moved from London to Northampton as one of the first families to do so. After the performance I told the director that I thought they had a hit on their hands. Here is the first announcement and description of the play as it was advertised at the time:

"How can Northampton become a New Town? It's been here a thousand years."

This is the main theme behind the play. It's the 1960s and Northampton is at a crossroads. The town's population is set to double as part of the government's New Towns Act. But as new estates welcome thousands of families from London and the old town centre undergoes radical changes, some fear Northampton's identity is being stripped away.

Tasked with Northampton's expansion over twenty momentous years, the newly formed Development Corporation will go to hilarious lengths to ensure targets are met – even adapting their radio jingle into a legendary pop record...

Made by local creatives and inspired by true events, ***60 Miles by Road or Rail*** *brings Northampton's extraordinary past and present crashing together to celebrate our hometown at a time when uncertainty threatens to pull us apart.*

It eventually had a week's run at the Theatre, although in my opinion, it wasn't the same script that I had previously seen and so much admired, and I was quite critical of it. I did tell the director at the time what I thought about this new version of the play, and he told me that I shouldn't be so critical, but I felt disappointed with the new format of the play, which had been altered quite a lot, and now had very little to do with the Northampton Development Corporation.

A scene from the Show '60 Miles by Road or Rail'

CHAPTER TEN

Becoming house-owners and moving house

Sometime after we'd settled into our house on the Lumbertubs Estate, the Government initiated a scheme whereby tenants could purchase their rented Council house under a new right-to-buy scheme, and so we decided to take up that opportunity. We were a little worried about not being able to afford the mortgage payments, but that didn't deter us from making inquiries.

We received the documentation soon after, and we decided that we would go ahead with the purchase of our property. And then something extraordinary happened to comfort us in our decision: I purchased a lottery ticket at the Weston Favell Shopping Centre in support of the Cobblers Football Club, and I won £1,000! With my winnings I bought a second-hand car, which delighted us all.

We become the proud owners of our house in Bitten Court in 1997, and both Rona and I were glad of our decision to purchase it. This proved to be a very happy period for all the family, and we took great pride in improving and decorating the house to suit our own tastes. I immediately set to work repainting the outside, and then made various improvements inside, while my two children, Jennifer and Heather, were growing-up in the house that we now owned. According to the contract we had signed, we were obliged to live in the house for at least five years.

We would eventually pay a total of £7,100 for the house, with our mortgage fixed at £40 per month over 25 years, a lot lower than in today's property market. We struggled a little at first, but always managed to find the money each month, and we continued living happily in that house for the next five years. Our two children were now both attending nearby schools, with Jennifer at Golding's Middle School and Heather at the Lumbertubs Primary School, and both were doing well at their respective schools. Rona had started to work again as a nurse at the Northampton General Hospital, while I continued working as caretaker at Lings Lower School, giving us the advantage of two salaries.

Rona, Jennifer and Heather in the garden

Then, in early 1985, we decided we'd like to move to a larger property, and so I began looking around in our area but could find nothing that seemed suitable for us. We wanted to remain in the Eastern District, because we'd now settled in and enjoyed living there. But one day I got talking with one of the teachers at my school, Steve Dunning, and he told me about a nice property he'd seen for sale in a private cul-de-sac on the Southfields Estate.

I went alone to look at the house, as Rona was working that day. On seeing the house, I immediately thought how much Rona would love it, although there would have to be quite a lot of improvements made. It would need a whole new central-heating system, as it still relied upon individual gas heaters. We had by now become so accustomed to our central heating in Lumbertubs, I couldn't imagine having to live without it. Another bad point was that the gardens were completely open, and so it would need new fencing all around. But I was very enthusiastic about the house itself and told the estate agent I was interested, and that we would most probably take it.

I rushed home excitedly and told Rona that I had reserved the house, but she wasn't too pleased with me about that before she had seen it. I told her that I was certain she too would love the house, and so we both went to look at it with the estate agent to show us all around. Rona pointed out how it was a lot smaller than our actual house, but I said that she'd quickly adapt and get used to it. In the end we finally agreed and set things in motion for the purchase of our new house. The house was priced at £29,500, with a mortgage of £80 per month. We thought this a lot of money for us to be paying at the time, although when compared with today's prices it does seem a small amount.

A short while after, the documents and contracts had all been read and signed, and we began with the preparations for our move. Both Heather and Jennifer were also really excited at the prospect of moving into a new house. Of course, there was a huge amount of packing to do, and it took quite some time, as we'd amassed so much furniture and all the other things necessary for a family of four. But we eventually got it all done, and I reserved a removal van for the day of our moving.

Once the van was loaded with all our stuff and we were about to leave our house for the final time, I looked at Rona and saw that she was crying, and I knew it was because she had grown to love our house on the Lumbertubs Estate. I reassured her as best I could that everything would be fine once we'd settled into the new house, and I hoped I was correct in assuming that. I too felt a pang as we drove off for the last time. We had forged a new life in that house over the years, and it is always difficult to change things so abruptly.

Our new house at Evesham Court, on the Southfields Estate, was only a ten-minute drive away from our old house, and it was nicely situated at the end of a quiet cul-de-sac. The removal men pulled up and set about unloading all our belongings and carrying them into the house for us, and it was soon done and ready for us to start unpacking and installing everything as we wished. Again, it turned into an exciting time for all of us once we began sorting and arranging everything, with the children gladly helping and joining in, and even Rona looked happy again as she arranged the kitchen and other places exactly as she wanted. She has always been a very house-proud person.

I was a little worried about the extra distance from this new house to the school where I worked, as I'd always walked the short distance from our old house. I had driven a few times, but soon noticed a few small incidents of damage to the car which was parked outside the school all day – there was no secure parking at that time – and so I decided to walk each day.

But once installed in our new house I purchased a bicycle, and so would cycle to work, which I continued to do for the rest of my time at that school. But once again, sadly, on two occasions my bicycle was stolen and had to be replaced.

I gradually became interested in serious cycling then and eventually bought myself a sports bike, which I would use at weekends, cycling at least 30 miles each time. I would cycle out into the countryside, taking a flask of coffee and sandwiches, and I'd often be gone for most of the day while Rona would be busy arranging and settling into the new house with our daughters. It was a great way for me to unwind after a full week at work.

We soon had a new central heating system fitted and erected a wooden fence around the property. I was told by one of the neighbours that the person who had lived there before us had sold part of our garden to one of the neighbours, which I thought a pity, as I would have liked a bigger garden, although it is still reasonably sized and very well laid out.

Heather & Jennifer

CHAPTER ELEVEN

My political life

During my time as caretaker at Lings Lower School I met many different teachers, one of whom, Mr. Schofield, introduced me to the local Labour Party, which would come to play a big part in my life. I also began helping the Thorplands Residents Association when it first got started, and it was quite satisfying to see the residents coming together.

Around the same time, I became interested in and helped with the formation of a local youth club at the Brookside Centre, which quickly became a great success. We received initial help from people in the Association of Youth Clubs, but after a few weeks they withdrew and left us to organise and run it on our own. But some of the young people who attended were pretty much out of control at times, and on one occasion they smashed a lot of the new equipment we'd raised funds for to purchase.

We also installed a sweet stall, where the young people could purchase sweets and other treats they enjoyed. An elderly woman came each week to help serve the sweets, and it soon became very popular and quite successful, making a small profit which helped towards the buying of new equipment. But we struggled to find volunteers to help run the youth club, and although we advertised locally for help from residents, we couldn't find enough volunteers to carry on with this venture. We did receive a lot of help from a teacher, Clive Ison, who was running another youth club at the Emmanuel Church. I still meet with him quite often, and he is still involved with helping young people. I was very sorry when our youth club closed, although the Residents Association is still going strong.

Shortly after this I joined the Labour Party, as Mr. Schofield had convinced me that I should. My association with the party lasted for thirty years, during which time I had a great many tribulations and many good moments. I met a lot of colleagues with whom I worked. I also met many of the Mayors of Northampton, although I didn't know then that one day in the future I too would become Mayor of Northampton.

By joining the Labour Party I gained a great deal of experience and self-confidence, as I'd always found it difficult to stand up and speak in public, and now even more so when speaking about politics, but I soon became more confident. One of my colleagues told me that if wanted to speak better at public meetings I should practice speaking while looking into a mirror, as do many actors to perfect their lines and interpretations. I did try this, but it wasn't of much help to me, as when I began speaking, I still felt nervous and would often get my words wrong or mixed up. But over time I did improve and slowly became a lot better at speaking at our meetings.

I was soon promoted onto the executive committee of the Northampton South Labour Party, and some of the members I met there taught me a great deal about politics. One colleague in particular, John Dickie, had a huge influence over my political journey, and I supported a lot of different fractions of the party which he advised me to join. I joined the Chile Solidarity Group, for whom I raised a lot of money, and John Dickie was very influential in running that group.

After serving on the executive for some time, I knew that I wanted to become a Councillor and serve my local community, but I was still not confident enough to stand for a safe seat. The first seat I stood for was the Welford Road Constituency, which was a safe Conservative seat, and so I had little chance of winning. The second seat I tried for was with the Kingsthorpe Labour Party, and I ran a good campaign, but it was won by Richard Church, who would later become Mayor of Northampton.

In later years I become quite friendly with Richard, and it was to him I turned when I decided to join the Liberal Democrat party, and he welcomed me. I began delivering the party newspaper around the constituency and was contacted shortly after by my good friend Chris Stranbra. Chris and I were on the county council together, the only two Liberal Democrat councillors elected at that time.

Chris eventually became leader of the Liberal Democrats, while I become deputy leader, and we worked together for many years. At the time, the Labour Party were in the opposition, and we asked a lot of questions and put forward many motions, quickly becoming a force to be reckoned with.

I eventually decided to try to become councillor of my own ward, which was at that time the Lumbertubs Ward where I was still living and working. I went through the selection process and was picked to represent the Labour Party. There were only ten members present, and I believed I had a fair chance of becoming a councillor

Unfortunately, at that time my depression had become quite acute again, and after being selected by a majority, I was nominated to stand as candidate for Lumbertubs. But then I decided I wouldn't accept the offer to represent Lumbertubs, nor become councillor if I was elected by the people. I was really all over the place with my depression at the time, and so I felt I had done the right thing by withdrawing my candidacy. I duly sent a letter to the executive committee stating that I was unable to accept the nomination. Tony Berry went on to represent the Lumbertubs Ward and became their councillor

Once when I was out campaigning with a West Midlands Labour representative, I asked him why the Labour Councillors in my ward reported a lot of things that needed looking at but then nothing was ever done, and he told me that it was because they wanted to keep those wards for the Labour Party, and if the districts were improved they might turn to the conservative party. I have never forgotten that.

I have always been a pacifist at heart, and I joined the C.N.D. and joined many protest marches for this country to give up its nuclear arsenal. I marched to Molesworth with Janet and Mike Thomas, and I met the women from Molesworth who were camping out to protest against the nuclear weapons. I took them food and other supplies to help support them, admiring their courage and commitment in this campaign.

We staged a great many social events to raise funds within the Labour Party, and I put my name to a motion which called for the finances of the North and South Labour Parties to be joined. I also ran the campaign for the M.P. Sally Keeble, who won the seat during the landslide victory of the Labour Party in the 1979 General Election under Tony Blair. I never did like that man, however, and always considered him to be a Tory in disguise.

I went to a meeting shortly after the landslide victory, and I asked Sally Keeble why so many members of the Labour Party were resigning, but she wouldn't answer my question and quickly changed the subject. By that time, I was already disappointed with the Labour Party and their policies, and I finally left them after thirty years when Tony Blair took our country into a war against Iraq. I never forgave them for that, and it ended my long association with them.

.

CHAPTER TWELVE

Heather's sporting achievements

My daughter, Heather, had been practicing rhythmic gymnastics from the age of five, and by the age of eleven she was a remarkably talented athlete. Under the guidance of Mrs. Belshaw, her coach, we took her to Leicester to compete in the under-13s International rhythmic gymnastics competition, with her group representing Great Britain. They won 1st prize, with each girl receiving a gold medal for their achievement. I felt immensely proud of my daughter, and throughout the years we supported her by taking her to different venues all around the country. She later presented me with her medal and asked me to look after it for her, which I have done with pride.

Heather, top left, with her winning team

Heather's sporting achievements made me think about my own lack of sporting efforts, and once when we went on holiday to the seaside and I had to watch all my family splashing about and swimming in the waves while all I could do was paddle close to the shore, I felt quite embarrassed at not being able to swim at the age of forty! I'd never been taught to swim as a child because of my traumatic upbringing.

I decided then that I must learn to swim, and I attended a six-week learning course at the Mounts Swimming Baths. On completing the course, I was able to swim quite well, and it was like a new beginning for me.

I then went to swim three times a week, and very soon was managing to swim 32 lengths of the pool each time, which was approximately half a mile. At the same time, I began attending a gym for other physical exercises, including weightlifting, building up my strength and stamina to a point where I felt really strong and healthy in my body.

Later, when I was in hospital with Covid, the consultant told me once that if I hadn't been going to the gym regularly and so reinforcing my body's natural resistance, I might not have survived.

CHAPTER THIRTEEN

Getting an allotment

Around this time, I decided that I'd like to have an allotment and so be able to grow a lot of my own fruit and vegetables. As a young boy, I had derived a lot of comfort and friendship through helping elderly people to look after their allotments, and the appeal was still attractive to me. I applied through the Northampton Borough Council and was allotted a plot on a site that had recently been transformed into allotments.

I began work on my allotment straight away, and quickly made a lot of like-minded friends. I also approached the committee and told them that I was the Councillor for the Talavera district, and as such I disposed of a fund known as the Councillors' Empowerment Money. From this fund I bought new equipment for the allotments, including a Rotavator and quite a lot of other tools, as well as a new concrete compound for the manure. The allotment secretary then asked me if I would like another plot to work on, and I readily agreed, as that would mean extra planting and harvests for me and my family. Shortly after that I was asked to join the committee.

I eventually served as Chairman Secretary, and I also ran the allotment shop, which I quickly transformed into a profit-making venture. During the winter, I loved nothing better than to sit outside in front of a blazing log fire with a mug of steaming hot tea, while slowly grilling burgers and sausages on an open fire. I quickly became self-sufficient with growing my vegetables, and I entered my allotment on two successive years for the best allotment prize staged by the Northampton Allotment Association. The prize-giving was held at the Conservative Club on St George's Avenue, and I attended the event with my good friends from the allotment, Roy and Margaret Palmer, who became secretary and chairman, and we all worked very closely together.

The chairman of the Association of Northampton Allotments announced the winners, and Mr. and Mrs. Palmer won first prize while I was awarded second prize, and this occurred on two occasions. Sadly, today they have stopped holding such shows, due to the lack of interest and low attendance of allotment holders.

Dennis & friends – barbecue at his allotment

During my tenure as secretary, I recruited over 150 people to join Southfield's Allotment Association, and Roy Palmer, who was then chairman, worked nonstop to improve the site and make sure it was always kept clean and tidy, until it was seen to be one of the finest allotments in Northampton. I was visited then by the allotment officer for the contractors at Northampton Borough

Council, who told me that our allotment was one of his best sites in Northampton. We were all highly pleased to hear this, and then we organised a few open days and shows which were very well attended. One time we invited the Mayor of Northampton, Councillor Tony Ansell, and the money we raised was given to his local charity, the Hope Center.

During this stage in my life, I decided that I'd also like to keep a few chickens, and so I made some enquiries and purchased four chickens, although that number quickly became twenty. I also wrote a weekly column for the Chronicle & Echo newspaper, in which my chickens were named after local politicians, and this went on for four years, until the paper stopped it. The column was called Afona, but I never did find out who edited it. But I had a lot of fun writing about chickens and people, and I really enjoyed what I was writing about.

I also built up a steady little business selling the eggs, which helped with the upkeep of the chickens.

I enjoyed looking after my hens, and I would sit in the pen and feed them by hand. Most of them had become like pets, and my wife also helped me to look after them. I also attended quite a few shows where we really enjoyed talking with other people who kept chickens. But then one morning when I went out to tend and feed my chickens, I found them all dead. I had forgotten to lock them in their roost overnight, and Mr. Fox had been on a rampage and killed them all. We were so upset, and when I began to clear up and dispose of the dead chickens, I knew I couldn't begin over again. So, I got rid of the chicken coop and revamped my garden, which today looks quite splendid.

Dennis, the outdoors man

CHAPTER FOURTEEN

Wilson…my dog

In 2012 we decided we would like to have a dog, preferably one that needed rehoming. We made enquiries and then travelled to Bedford, where we were shown around a dog rehoming establishment. I spotted straightaway a small puppy, just six months old, and was told it was a male crossbreed between a Jack Russell and a Border Terrier. It was jumping up and down against the mesh of its kennel and caught my eye from the start. I told the keeper that we'd take that one, as it seemed to have chosen me, and that was the beginning of a long relationship.

As my true name would have been Dennis Wilson had I been named after my biological father, I decided to call our new puppy Wilson. A lot of people then asked me if I'd named him after our ex-Prime Minister, Harold Wilson. One of the staff from the rehoming kennels came to visit us at home to assess if it would be suitable for re-homing Wilson. She found no problems and told us we could have him to come and live with us. I was so excited about having my own dog again.

After signing the adoption papers, we brought him home and named him Wilson. He very quickly became part of our family, and I would take him for a walk every morning. We also had some good times with him on holiday, and he always knew Hunstanton as soon as he got there. He really loved it. We had to be careful with him when we were near other people, though, as he wasn't very friendly around strangers and showed off quite a bad temper. We used to warn people who wanted to stroke him or fuss over him that he wasn't a friendly dog, and that they should be careful. The vet once told me it was probably because of a trauma he'd experienced as a puppy, and that if it hadn't been for us nobody else would have been willing to rehome him.

We'd often take Wilson to visit our neighbours, Pat and John Robbins, who lived in a house opposite us, and he quickly got to know them and was always well-behaved. We were also very friendly with them, and we often went on different trips with them. John was quite an eccentric character and would dress-up in all kinds of different outfits, but we really enjoyed being friends with them.

Sadly, both John and Pat had to move into a care home in Wellingborough. John is now totally bedridden and hasn't left his bed for over a year and is understandably very depressed. Their daughter and son-in-law live in Cornwall and so find it very difficult to visit them. Rona still visits them regularly and takes them magazines and other necessary things, but it is very sad for us to see them now, quite unable to look after themselves. But Rona talks with them about different places we used to visit together and helps to lift their spirits a little.

Wilson lived with us for thirteen years, becoming a true friend and companion, and then we had to say goodbye to him as he began suffering from so many different ailments. We miss him terribly, as he'd been part of our family life for so long and we'd had so many good times with him. We held a short prayer service for him in our back garden, with a few friends and neighbours joining us, and so now he has a permanent flowery grave there. He is still always with us in our memories, and my friend, Peter Dietrich, (more about him later) a poet and author, wrote a fitting elegy for Wilson which I read out in his memory:

IN OUR HEARTS

For Wilson

We thought of you today,
But that is nothing new;
We thought about you yesterday
And days before that, too;
We think of you in silence,
We often speak your name,
Now all we have are memories
And your picture in a frame;
But your memory is our keepsake
With which we'll never part;
God has you in his keeping…
…we have you in our heart.

I will never forget my little dog Wilson, and even as I am writing this piece, I can feel a lump in my throat. Wilson made me so happy for so long, but I still have a lot of wonderful memories and photos.

CHAPTER FIFTEEN

My prodigal children

One evening I answered an unexpected phone call, and a woman's voice asked me if I was Mr. Dennis Meredith, and if I had a son named Kenneth. I answered yes, but that he had lived with his adoptive parents for many years now. I asked who was speaking, and she told me that she was the wife of Kenneth Raines, who was my son, and that they lived in Hampshire. She went on to say that he would like to have some contact with me, and would I be happy if he wrote me a letter telling me a little about himself, and then perhaps he could come to visit me. I was quite taken aback by all this at the time, but I told her that of course he could write to me, and I would be very glad to find out more about him and how his life had evolved.

(*Readers of the first volume of my autobiography will have read about the reasons why my son had been adopted when very young, and why I'd decided to let his foster parents eventually adopt him as their own child.)*

A few days later I received a handwritten letter from him in which he told me a little about himself. From this I learnt that he was now married and living in Hampshire, and that he had two children named Kristy and Holly. He still lived on the farm where he had been brought up by his foster parents, with whom he seemed to have had a good and lasting relationship. He told me that they'd brought him up as a true country boy, but now both had passed away. I had met his foster mother when I visited a few times before he was adopted, and I found her to be a typical farmer's wife, full of life and energy, and I knew right away that my son would be well looked after with such people.

I replied to his letter and told him that I'd be very happy to meet him and suggested that he visit us in Northampton and so meet my own family. I didn't know what to expect, but then one weekend he arrived with his wife, Tina, and their two children, my grandchildren. My first impression was of how much he resembled me as a young man, a true lookalike. He seemed quite reserved and kept staring hard at me, as though trying to fathom me out. It was a strange feeling for me, and I felt there was no bonding between us, which I told myself was understandable, as he'd been a small boy at our last meeting. But it was good to meet his wife and children on that first visit.

Dennis with his son Kenneth

We agreed to stay in touch with each other and this went on for about two years. We visited him in Hampshire on several occasions, and he always made us very welcome. But after a while he told us that he'd split with his wife and children, and that she was now in a new relationship, while he was living in a different area in Hampshire. We visited him then at his new home and met his new wife, who was very kind to us, and we got on very well. We went out for lunch together at a local pub, and we all really enjoyed it as his new wife told us all about herself.

Ken told us about what he was now doing for a living, working in a forest and making charcoal. He said it was a dirty job but quite well paid at the time. I found I was getting on with him a lot better now, and we started to talk about the future. We sometimes took my granddaughters our for a day and had some great times together. Kristy was 9 and Holly was 8 at the time. Once he told me that he'd like to change his name back to my surname again, but I told him it wouldn't be a good idea now as his children were already used to his name, and he accepted that.

We visited him a few more times, although his visits to us slowly got scarcer and then stopped altogether. I telephoned him a few times to see if he still wanted to meet with us, but I have had no correspondence from him now for a very long time and he doesn't answer any of my e-mails or phone calls.

My daughter Jennifer, Kenneth's sister, also contacted him, but I don't know if she is still in touch with him as she has chosen to make her own way in life without the support of her family. The last time I met with her was about two years ago, and she told me that she had contacted her birthmother, my first wife, Barbara, who had left me alone with the two children when I was still living in Basingstoke.

She then showed me a picture of her mother, but I no longer recognised her. Jennifer also told me that she'd visited her mother on several occasions, but without me knowing. I had never discussed with Jennifer about what had occurred between myself and her mother all those years ago, and I was no longer interested in her. I could never forgive how she had left me alone with the two children, with Jennifer just three years old and Kenneth a mere three weeks old.

Jennifer also decided that she would no longer call Rona her mum anymore, and Rona was truly upset by this. She never said anything, but I know she was deeply hurt. I don't know for sure if this was because she had met her birthmother and listened to her story, but whatever the reason, she also chose not to stay in touch with me. But I often think about her and wonder how she is getting on with her own three children. I have had no contact with her for the past two years, nor with my grandchildren. I don't think I would even recognise them now were they to walk past me, and that makes me very sad, but we all have to accept the situations that unroll around us.

I have recently tried to renew contact with my son Kenneth and my two grandchildren, Kristy and Holly, but they seem to have chosen not to respond in any way. I must accept this as a part of my life, no matter how sad it makes me feel.

My other daughter, Heather, has always remained close to us. She now has two children, Luke and Emily, and we are all in regular contact, which is a comfort to me. Of course, I do understand that all children need to quit the family home eventually to set out on their own paths in life, as I did at the very young age of sixteen. But I think it is always a bit of a wrench for parents when it happens, and that is also why it is a great comfort for them to have close contact with their grandchildren. Now I really do enjoy seeing them and following them as they begin their own lives.

Rona, Dennis, Emily, Luke (with Molly) & Heather

CHAPTER SIXTEEN

My depression and dyslexia

I have suffered from an anxiety-based depression for most of my life, and it has been a sometimes-devastating force which I have had to cope with from when I was a young boy at school. Depression is not simply feeling unhappy about certain things, but it has other far-reaching symptoms such as feeling tired and unwell and being unable to concentrate on anything. It has affected my whole working life.

The worst part about my depression as an adult was that I truly believed that most people in my life were against me, and especially the headteachers in the school where I worked as caretaker. Whenever I was going through a particularly bad attack my paranoia grew worse, and I would shut myself away in my office so as not to have to speak with anyone. But in all my thirty years of working at that school, I never told a soul that I suffered severely from depression.

There was still quite a stigma surrounding depression when I was growing up, and people with depression were simply told to pull themselves together, me included, although it was impossible to do that when it took hold of you. It was a misunderstood affliction until quite recently. I did try a lot of different aids to help with my depression over the years, but none of them worked on a permanent basis. I even undertook trials for different companies who produced different remedies to fight off depression, although again none of them worked for me. The only thing that did help me a little was a lightbox which I would sit in front of for about an hour each day.

I did manage to get on top of my darker feelings towards the end of my working life, and then I made an appointment with a psychiatrist and told her about my long history of depression. She told me that, in her opinion, mine was a classic case of depression, and that she would try to help me become a different and less anxious person. She went on to say that my depression was most probably rooted in my traumatic childhood, which I told her about, and now, looking back again and writing about it here, I think she was right.

She prescribed antidepressant tablets, explaining to me that they weren't addictive and would help me a great deal, and so I have been taking antidepressants now for fifteen years. They have made such a difference to my life, and although I do still get occasional bouts of depression, they are nowhere near as violent as they used to be. It has been a very long struggle, but I'm happy to say that I have come through it now with the help of my wife and my family.

Another mental ailment that has been with me throughout my life is dyslexia. Dyslexia is a learning disorder that involves reading difficulties due to problems identifying speech sounds and learning how they relate to letters and words (decoding). Also known as a reading disability, dyslexia is a result of individual differences in areas of the brain that process language. Dyslexia can be very debilitating, and it also caused many problems for me throughout my working life. And once again it was a problem I was ashamed of, and so I kept it hidden from all those around me.

I didn't know I had dyslexia as a child, nor even what it was, like most people at the time. I simply accepted that I couldn't spell or read properly, and later I would always blame it on my school, thinking that I hadn't been properly educated nor received the extra help I needed. But of course, when I was at school dyslexia was still a mostly unknown ailment, and so most teachers simply put it down to learning difficulties or laziness in any child suffering from it.

Years later, when caretaker of a school, I had to write regular reports for the school governors concerning building fabrics and other materials used in my work, and later as site supervisor. This created enormous problems for me, as my writing was so bad, and the only way I could get round this was to dictate letters and reports to my wife, who would write them out correctly for me. Without her help I would have found it difficult to carry on as caretaker, because over time I had to write ever more reports, until it reached a stage where my job meant writing almost as much as all my other tasks. At that time, computers weren't yet much in use in schools, and even if I'd had one, I wouldn't have known how to use it. I was also made health and safety officer for the school, which only added to my writing duties.

I eventually contacted an adult learning unit at one of our local schools, and soon after a representant visited me at home. She was very kind and understanding, and after I told her about my dyslexia and the writing difficulties it caused me at work, she asked me to write a short essay in my own style. I must confess that I felt highly embarrassed, but she reassured me and told me not to worry. I wrote an essay about my garden, as I was a very keen gardener and knew quite a lot about gardening. She read what I'd written, and then spoke to me at great length about it. She then told me that if, as a child, I'd received the help that dyslexic pupils now receive in schools, I may well have gone on to university to get a degree.

I was overjoyed to hear that, and then she invited me to attend some courses at her school to learn a lot more about dyslexia. I was also interested in learning more about computers, and she told me about a certain computer program that could help me with my dyslexia. It was named Dragon Drop, and it allowed you to dictate directly into the computer and it would automatically type your dictation, leaving a visual copy of your notes on the screen to read and correct. This has been a huge help to me over the years, and it shows how much this modern technology can be a useful resource.

I decided after that to always speak out about my dyslexia and depression, and if I wrote something and people would point out my mistakes and criticise me, I would explain to them that I am dyslexic and so they shouldn't criticise my writing or spelling mistakes, as it isn't my fault.

I have now managed to overcome both my dyslexia and my depression, and the help and encouragement I received has enabled me to write this book, as well as to help many other people who suffer from the same afflictions. I have been contacted by a lot of people in a similar dilemma, suffering from depression or dyslexia, and I have helped them as best I can to overcome their problems. Many of them then write to thank me for the help I gave them, and I reply that it is part of my job, and that they should just get on with their lives as best they can. But if you do suffer from acute depression, my advice would be to always seek professional help.

CHAPTER SEVENTEEN

My market stall and car-boot sales

While working as caretaker at Lings Lower School, I wanted to branch out more into other activities and so earn more money for my growing family needs. I already had several cleaning jobs in and around Northampton, and I also looked after the garden of a local businessman. He ran a professional cleaning company in Northampton, and so I enrolled to do several cleaning jobs for him.

I got to know another caretaker on those jobs, and we became friendly. Then after a few discussions, we thought it would be a good idea to start our own cleaning business. We were both ambitious, and we both wanted to go into business.

We printed flyers advertising our services and delivered them to a lot of different companies, but we didn't get a lot of response and so we decided it might be better to try our luck in market-trading. I contacted the market in Rushden, and they agreed to rent us a stall. We started by selling second-hand goods which we purchased from jumble-sales and unused stock sales, and our stall was quickly doing quite well.

Sometime later I purchased six brand-new dresses at a bargain price and which I thought should make a decent profit, and I took them to my partner's house to store them until our next market day. But when I went to collect them, he informed me that he'd already given three of the dresses to his family. When I asked about the money he'd got for them, he told me that as it was for his family he hadn't charged them!

I was quite annoyed by this, and it spelt the end of our partnership. I kept it going on my own for about four weeks, and then I decided to give up the stall, as it was too much for me to handle alone along with all my other part-time jobs. I then came up with the idea of having a car-boot sale, as they were proving very popular with the public.

I gathered all my stock from the market and set about selling it at different car-boot sales, and I was soon doing very well and wanted to take it further. So, I started buying and selling old toys from jumble sales, which I then repaired to resell, and business was quickly flourishing. I was busy all the time at first, but then a few of the other car-bootees caught on and started selling toys as well, and that was the end of my car-boot sale days. But things had been going well for me during this time, and my financial status was now a lot better.

Around the same time, we decided to try out a camping holiday with our children, and so I visited a local camping shop and bought all the equipment we might need. I did have some great times camping with my family, but on our first excursion we hadn't a clue of how to put up a tent! On arriving at the camp site, we had real difficulties setting up our tent, but luckily for us there was a family nearby who gladly came to help us.

I quickly discovered that there is a great sense of fraternity among campers, and it certainly helped us through our novice stage. We were a bit naive to begin with, and we hadn't thought about buying a lamp so that we could see inside the tent at night. We spent a good part of our first day walking around the shops trying to find one where we could buy a camping lamp, and we did eventually find one. But then on that first night we discovered that we didn't really need one, as it didn't get dark before 10 o'clock and we were already getting ready for bed. But we all enjoyed the camping experience from the start and spent most of our future holidays and weekends camping.

On one occasion we planned to visit a camp site in Dorset, and so set off in our car with the children and all our camping gear. But the car broke down on the way, and I had to walk and find the nearest garage, which was quite a few miles away. There were two mechanics working there, and they drove me back to the car and my waiting family, who were pleased to see us.

They soon fixed the problem and got the car running again, and when I asked them how much I owed them they told me not to worry, but to go on and enjoy our holiday. We all thanked them profusely for such kindness, and that cheered us during the rest of the drive.

Rona, Jennifer & Heather & the car in front of the tent

All the family soon took to camping

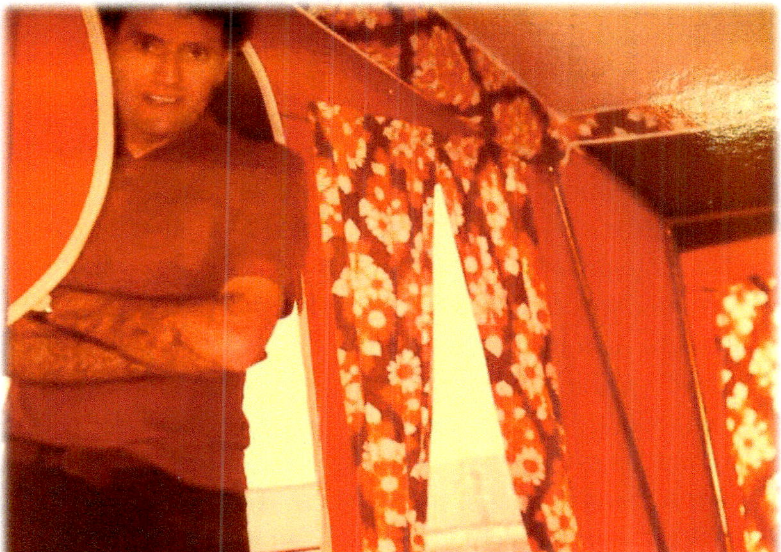

We eventually purchased a fixed caravan on a camping site in Bedford, and we'd visit and stay over most weekends for many years. It was frequented mostly by young families like ours, and we made a lot of good friends over time while joining in a lot of different social events.

There were many sports facilities available, and Rona and I enjoyed playing the French game of pétanque, which is similar to our own bowling games. We quickly became quite skilled, and once entered a national competition and finished as runner-up. We were also once invited to Germany to take part in an international competition, but I had far too many work commitments and so, unfortunately, we couldn't go.

Our involvement with the site grew and deepened the more we visited, and we became very close friends with a lot of other regular visitors as we grew to know them better. We become particularly friendly with one couple, Sheila and Derek, and we eventually went on a holiday to Jamaica with them. We had a fantastic time, and it was one of the best holidays I've ever had.

I started horse-riding with Sheila, something I'd never tried before, but I found I enjoyed it and was quite confident and successful after a few trials. On another occasion I asked Sheila if she'd like to go on an offshore canoe trip with me, and she agreed. We'd paddled out quite a way from the shore when I suddenly felt an acute pain in my side and was forced to stop paddling. I could no longer handle or steer the canoe, and I told Sheila she'd have to paddle us back to shore, but she said in a panic that she didn't know how to do that. I thought then that the safest way was for me to jump over the side and to swim back to the shore, pulling the canoe behind me. So, I did this and discovered that the water barely came up to my knees! We both burst out laughing, and I have never forgotten that incident.

I have kept in touch with some of our friends from the caravan site, and we sometimes go out for dinner and talk about the good times we spent together with our families. At one point I was asked if I would like to run the refreshment kiosk on the site, and I agreed. We began offering lunches and tea and coffee, and it quickly became popular and successful, and we made a lot of money for the site which went towards improving the grounds.

Eventually, I had to sell my caravan because my increasing commitments as a Councillor left me little spare time, but it was an experience that I will never forget. Also, my children were growing up. Jennifer was now married with three children, while Heather was living with her partner, Bob Jones, and they had one child, my grandson Luke. Unfortunately, their relationship didn't last, and Heather now has a new partner with whom she has another child, Emily, my granddaughter. Both Luke and Emily are doing well.

CHAPTER EIGHTEEN

School Governor

While still working as caretaker at Lings School, I unexpectedly became a governor at Blackthorns Lower School. It was around the time I met my good friend Maurice O'Neill, who was a headteacher at one of the local middle schools in Northampton. At that time the Labour Party had taken control of the County Council, and the party ratio of school governors was to be increased.

I attended a meeting at which there were four representatives of the Conservative Party and four Labour Party representatives. Maurice O'Neill proposed me to be chairman. The vote took place, and it was a drawn tie, and so the meeting had to be postponed. But at the next meeting the Conservatives agreed that I could be elected as chairman, while one of the Conservatives would be vice-chairman. We all accepted that decision, and so I become chairman of the governors at Blackthorns Lower school.

I remained a governor at that school for twelve years, and it turned out to be quite a demanding position. I had a great many responsibilities, including the interviewing of candidates for positions as teachers, and I also interviewed two candidates for the position of Head Teacher of the school. I told myself that this was no small accomplishment for a working-class boy from London.

On one occasion one small boy had an accident in the swimming pool and sadly died, and this affected me greatly as chairman of the school. Some of the governors went around the Blackthorn

Estate to collect money to help the family pay for his funeral. It was a tragic occasion for everyone concerned, and for the whole school.

But I mostly enjoyed my time as chairman at the school, and I worked very closely with the Headteacher, Mrs. Joy Prescott. When I eventually retired as chairman of the Governors, the school held a moving assembly for me, and they presented me with a nice suitcase. Very fitting, I told myself, as it seemed a good time for me to move on.

CHAPTER NINETEEN

Another new direction

I decided to retire as a caretaker after thirty-two years working at the same school. I applied for an early retirement, because a private cleaning business, **Amy Cleaning**, was taking over the cleaning of the county's schools from the County Council, who had been running the service for such a long time, and I didn't want to work for a private company.

There was a tremendous leaving party given in my honour in the school hall, to which I invited my family and many friends. A lot of effort had been made by the school's PA officer who organised the event, and many former teachers with whom I had worked were invited. The headteacher, Mrs. Sutcliffe, made a moving speech and wished me all the very best for the future. But it was also a sad and moving moment for me, leaving after thirty-two years of working at that school. At the end of the party, I was taken home in a car provided by the local radio station who had attended and interviewed me. I also had a great many gifts to transport from so many different people.

A little while later I was approached by the chief executive of the Amy Cleaning company, who asked me if I would be interested in joining them to give advice on setting up the new contract with school caretakers. I decided to try it out, as I was already missing my daily work as caretaker at the school, and this would help me ease into my full retirement. I was engaged as a supervisor because of my lengthy cleaning experience at the school, and it turned out to be quite a challenging role. But I carried out my duties as best I could, and I think I left a lasting impression.

I helped a great many school caretakers to integrate into the new company that was now going to take over the cleaning tasks in Northampton schools. It was challenging, as most of the caretakers were accustomed to working for the County Council, and now they had to become employees of Amy Cleaning. Some things would be slightly different with their working conditions, but I had to convince them that most things would remain as they had been with the County Council.

Things got off on a good footing, and for a time everything went well. But when a new chief executive took over, I noticed that things were changing and began to go downhill. I was called into his office one day and he asked me why I was on a higher salary than he was. I explained that I was hired on a freelance basis and so was working a great many hours, which was reflected in the money I took home. If he wanted me to earn less than him, he should cut down my hours of work. But then when they hired a new catering manager with whom I didn't get on very well, I decided to leave the company. This wasn't what I wanted in my retirement.

At the same time, I had become interested in the Liberal Democrat Party, as it was the only party not to support the war in Iraq when Tony Blair had been Prime Minister. I decided then to leave the Labour Party and joined the Liberal Democrats, which is still the party I support today. I believed in their policies and their fairness towards the electorate, and they seemed to listen to the ordinary people's concerns. Then, after eighteen months of campaigning in the Talavera District, I managed to win the election and became a Liberal Democrat Councillor for the Borough Council of Northampton. I had achieved my ambition to become a Councillor, which I hadn't done while with the Northampton Labour Party.

The Liberal Democrats eventually took control of the Council, and I served on the planning committee for a good number of years, and then served on the scrutiny committee, where I saw through quite a lot of commitments. I achieved many good targets while serving as a Borough Councillor, and with my wife's help we would deliver leaflets to the residents of my constituency informing them of everything we were trying to achieve in the area.

I gained a great deal of experience while working with the planning committee, and I thoroughly enjoyed my time as a County Council Councillor. But then under the reorganisation of the Councils in Northampton, the government commissioners recommended the abolishment of the Northampton Borough Council, which would first become the Northampton Town Council, and then the West Northants Council. I then received the honour of being made an Honorary Alderman by the old Borough Council, and a little later I was nominated by the Conservatives on the Borough Council to become the Deputy Mayor of Northampton in 2021. It goes without saying, I was more than pleased and honoured to receive both these awards.

CHAPTER TWENTY

Fighting Covid

Many people will remember the year 2020 as the year the world underwent its worst pandemic in a very long time. The Covid-19 virus began circulating in the U.K. in early 2020, arriving primarily from travel elsewhere in Europe. Various sectors responded, with more widespread public health measures incrementally introduced from March 2020. The first wave was at the time one of the world's largest outbreaks. By mid-April the peak had been passed and restrictions were gradually eased. A second wave began in the autumn and peaked in mid-January 2021 and was deadlier than the first. The UK started a Covid-19 vaccination program in early December 2020. Generalised restrictions were gradually lifted and were mostly ended by August 2021.

Unfortunately, I caught the Covid virus and quickly became very ill. I was rushed to hospital by ambulance as I couldn't breathe normally, and I spent 36 hours in the accident and emergency department in a special cubicle for Covid patients. At that time the hospital was overrun with Covid patients.

I was then moved to the Covid emergency isolation ward and immediately given oxygen and antibiotics. After seven days I was informed I was well enough to return home. But 24 hours later I was back in hospital and given more oxygen and antibiotics. When reassessed by a doctor, he informed me that I was well enough to return home again. Then, three days later, Rona called an ambulance for me to return once more to the hospital, where my condition deteriorated rapidly. I asked the consultant if I was going to die, and he said not if he could help it!

I remained seriously ill throughout my stay at the hospital, with the worst thing being not allowed any visitors because of the new Covid restriction rules. My medication consisted of a great many antibiotics and steroids.

The man in the next bed was also very ill, more so than me, and I sensed that he might be dying as I could hear the beep of his monitor becoming gradually slower. When he did stop breathing, I couldn't hold back my tears. I was told he had a wife and three children whom he hadn't been allowed to see because of the visiting restrictions. When the nurse came to ask me if I was all right and why I was crying, I told her it was because there was nobody there to cry for him now. I also wondered if I would be next.

This was a very sad and worrying time for me, and especially when a priest came to administer the last rites. He said he would like to share a communion with me, and I readily agreed. But when he opened his hostia container, he found he only had one communion wafer left, which he said was very strange, whereas I thought to myself how lucky I had been!

A few days later the consultant came to tell me that there was only one more antibiotic which they could give me, and if this didn't have the required effect, I could expect the worst. Mercifully, it did appear to work. The same consultant then prescribed me with 150 steroids, which in turn had a very bad effect upon me. I suffered a psychotic attack, which in turn caused me to have a complete mental breakdown. I thought I was locked up in a prison and that I had to break out. I tried to open the door but it was locked with a security lock and so I couldn't open it.

I accused all the nurses of killing their patients, and I called to the police nine times and asked them to arrest my wife as she had stolen my car. I then locked myself into the toilet and refused to come out. Eventually the nurses had to call the security guards to get me out and try to contain me, while I recounted all kinds of delirious mumbo-jumbo. They eventually called a psychiatrist who came to speak with me, and they managed to get me back into my bed. But it needed six people to hold me down while they gave me an injection, and after the injection I decided I would make myself a nuisance.

I still had my phone near me, and so I played the Bob McFerrin song: **DONT WORRY - BE HAPPY** as loudly as I could, over and over, wanting to disturb every one of the poor nurses who were there to look after us all. I even heard one of them say that it was her favourite tune! Shortly after that I fell asleep from the effect of the injection, and the following morning I woke to find all my bedding on the floor, and I was drenched with sweat.

I called the nurse over and asked her what had happened to me, as I couldn't remember anything. She told me all about my uncontrollable behaviour, my unfounded accusations against the hospital staff and my frantic calls to the police, and then she added that I should also apologise to my wife, who had been so worried about me.

I discovered later that the steroids they had been giving me often cause people to suffer psychotic episodes, and that was what had happened to me. It really hadn't been my fault. I think they learnt a lot from my case regarding the steroids and the amount that I had been given, and hopefully they would monitor them more closely in the future.

About two weeks after this episode, I was finally given the all-clear to be discharged and to return home, but at the time I still couldn't walk and had to use a wheelchair. When the nurse pushed me out to meet my wife, all the staff lined the ward to cheer and clap me goodbye. I was absolutely delighted, and I couldn't thank them enough as the tears rolled down my sunken cheeks.

The overworked staff and doctors at the Northampton General Hospital had saved my life, and I owe them a gratitude that I will never forget. It took me another 18 months to fully recover from my Covid infection, and I was diagnosed with what they termed Long Covid.

It was indeed a terrible time for all of us, that year of the Covid pandemic, and so many people and families suffered and were affected by the loss of loved ones. But we did come through it in the end, and it also brought out the community spirit of old again, which I feel was not a bad thing.

CHAPTER TWENTY-ONE

Becoming Mayor

I think that the biggest achievement in my life must be when I was elected to become the 782nd Mayor of Northampton, in 2022, at the age of 80. My wife, Rona, was elected with me as Mayoress. At the time, this was reported in the local press as here:

'A retired school caretaker has been named as the 782nd Mayor of Northampton and only the second appointed by the new town council. Mr Meredith was born in Islington but moved to Northampton in 1972. He was the caretaker at Lings Primary School for three decades before retiring, becoming a councillor, and is currently a Liberal Democrat member on West Northamptonshire Council. During his political career, he has been responsible for setting up youth clubs and resident associations across Northampton.

Meredith and his Mayoress, Rona, celebrated their golden wedding anniversary last year, enjoying two children and two grandchildren. Cllr Meredith is an avid gardener with a passion for his allotment, campaigning tirelessly in his ward for allotment space and is always keen to support those with green fingers.

His two chosen charities are St Vincent De Paul and The Army Benevolent Fund, a Soldiers Charity, both of which work nationwide and locally, tackling issues such as loneliness, supporting veterans as well as serving military personnel.'

Both myself and Rona really enjoyed our year of being Mayor and Mayoress. I received a huge amount of support from my civic assistant, Miss Lizzie Hawkins, who revealed herself to be quite brilliant when helping to write my speeches and organising all the events I had to attend as mayor. I also had a wonderful chauffeur, Mr David Peach, who drove the Mayoral car while taking us to the many events. Over the year we attended hundreds of different events, making it impossible for me to recall all of them, but each one was special in its own way, and here I will mention a few that have stayed in my mind for one reason or another.

I recall one occasion when we attended a Beer Festival in Beckets Park, and one woman appeared to be a bit the worse for drink and tried to take the mayoral gold chain from around my neck. David had to quickly intervene and diplomatically lead her away. The Mayoral chauffeur must also act as a bodyguard, and David looked after me brilliantly, so I can't thank him enough.

I also visited the Prince's Trust, a United Kingdom-based charity founded in 1976 by King Charles III, (then Prince of Wales) to help vulnerable young people get their lives on track. It supports 11-to-30-year-olds who are unemployed or struggling at school and at risk of exclusion. Many of the young people helped by the trust face issues such as homelessness, disability, mental health problems, or trouble with the law.

I was very impressed with the work they undertake to help the young people, who participate in different courses for 12 weeks. At the end of each course, they all seem proud of what they have learnt and achieved, which usually makes a huge difference to their future lives. I had the great pleasure of presenting them with their signed certificates, and I wished them all the best of luck for the future. I was also told by the organiser of the trust that some of the young people had already managed to find jobs which was a truly remarkable achievement considering what some of them had been through already in their young lives.

I had early on become known as the 'Dancing Mayor', as I can't resist the appeal of music, and on one occasion I visited a group of young people afflicted with Down syndrome. There was a disco at the event, and I quickly managed to get them all up and dancing along with me, but then they wouldn't let me sit down for even one minute, as they all wanted me to dance with them.

At another event, a senior citizens' party for the 2nd anniversary of their social meeting-place in Duston, I met a lady of 102 years. Her daughter informed me that she still lived alone in her own home and still did all her own shopping and housework. Incredible stamina, which put me somewhat to shame at my tender age of 80!

When the band struck up a lively waltz, I approached this lady and asked if she would like to dance with me, and she readily agreed. We had a jolly dance together, with her laughing and very nimble on her feet, and I think that's where my title of the dancing Mayor originally came from, although I danced on all occasions whenever music was part of the event.

There were so many other organisations and events that I visited, totalling 390 in all during my year as Mayor, and so it would be impossible for me to list them all here. But one of the most solemn occurred when I was absent on holiday, and I had to return immediately to carry out my Mayoral duties. This was when Queen Elizabeth II passed away, and I returned to Northampton to attend a special church service at All Saints church, in the town centre. It was a very sad occasion, as she had been our Queen and head of state for so long, it just seemed impossible that she had left us. Many in the congregation shed tears in her memory, me included.

At the same time, I think I was the only Mayor to attend in quick succession the Queen's Jubilee celebrations, followed by her funeral service, and then, immediately after, the new King's ascension to the throne and finally his Coronation Celebrations. I had to read out the proclamation for the new King, Charles III, from the steps of the Guildhall, and when I'd completed the official proclamation, I made a grave mistake by inviting everyone present to come to the Mayor's Parlour and join me for coffee. I was more than glad that most didn't take me up on the offer, as there must have been at least two thousand people there! The officers present told me I shouldn't have done that, as they had nowhere near enough cups, but as only about fifty people joined me for coffee it turned out all right in the end.

Mayoral Photo Diary by Peter Dietrich

During my tenure as Mayor, I had the constant services of a personal photographer, Peter Dietrich, whom I'd met shortly before becoming Mayor, and he was regularly with us taking photos at most of my public engagements. He is a widely travelled professional photographer and filmmaker, as well as a talented poet and author, and he produced a brilliant photo-album for me to celebrate and remember my year as Mayor of Northampton. I am truly indebted to him for his time and his patience, and we have since become very close friends. He has also been of great assistance in editing and proofreading the first volume of my autobiography, and now also this second volume. But more about that later.

Another highlight of my Mayoral duties was being invited to Marburg, in Germany. Marburg and Northampton have been twinned cities since October 1990. I had to seek the permission of the Lord-Lieutenant of Northamptonshire to accept this invitation, and he readily agreed. He thought it would be good for me to visit as representant of the town.

As my wife couldn't attend with me, my daughter, Heather, accompanied me on this visit, and the trip was a huge success. We stayed for five days in a local hotel, during which time we visited a great many different sites and attended official events, while being thoroughly looked after.

Marburg is a German town north of Frankfurt. It's home to Philipps University, founded in 1527. The Altstadt, or old town, includes half-timbered houses and the hilltop Landgrafenschloss, a castle with exhibits on sacred art and regional history. Bars and cafes line Marktplatz square and the narrow streets surrounding it. The 13th-century, Gothic-style St. Elizabeth's Church holds a shrine with the saint's remains.

I was greatly impressed by this town, and it struck me as being spotlessly clean and well looked-after. We also had two wonderful people looking after us, Chris and Christine, who made us feel very welcome, and even invited us to their home for dinner. Looking at the town was like looking at a picture book sometimes, and I hope to return on a visit sometime soon.

Chris & Christina with Dennis – Northampton Park in Marburg

My daughter represented the Northampton Town Council as my consort, which she did superbly, and I'm sure the Council would have been proud of her, as I was. She conducted herself very well, and the people of Marburg took to her immediately and made her welcome.

Dennis and daughter Heather in Marburg

On returning to Northampton the preparations for King Charles' coronation were underway, and once again I felt honoured and pleased to be able to officiate as Mayor of Northampton. It was a wonderful once-in-a-lifetime experience.

My year as Mayor just seemed to fly by, and very soon it was time for me to step down and hand over my duties to the incoming Mayor. This was a solemn and sad occasion, of course, but also a relief in that I would no longer be obliged to attend so many events and duties, which were tiring for someone of my age. But I had no regrets, and during the ceremony I was proud to announce that over the course of my year as Mayor I had collected a total of over £14,000 for my two chosen charities, which was something of a record.

Since retiring as Mayor, such a lot of people have stopped me to tell me how popular I had been, always ready to join in any event, anywhere, and some told me that in their opinion I had been the best Mayor they had known in office. I am proud and happy to know that I had this effect on the people I represented, and I remain proud of all my achievements as Mayor.

Dennis & Rona's inauguration

First Civic Ball at the Guildhall

Dennis joining musicians at a Civic Dinner

Dancing with a 'young' lady of 102 years old!

Drawing a raffle with assistant Lizzie

Scaling the heights at All Saints Church for Oak Apple Day

Solemn march from the Guildhall on Remembrance Day

Posing at a summer party in Abington Park

Another fund-raising raffle at a local restaurant

Serious moments in the Mayor's Parlour

Welcoming Ukrainian refugees at a reception

Rona planting a rowan tree in Abington Park

Celebration of King Charles III's Coronation

Final day as Mayor & Mayoress of Northampton

CHAPTER TWENTY-TWO

Some of my achievements

Looking back over my life after settling in Northampton, I can tell myself with some satisfaction that I have achieved a great many positive things over the years. Not least was the publishing of the first volume of my autobiography, **MY LIFE...THE WAY I SEE IT**. It has had quite a successful reception, and I hope it will help people who find that things aren't going well for them to fight back against any adversity and learn from my own experiences that anything can be achieved if you are determined enough. That was my primary aim in writing that book, and now this second volume.

But one of the biggest challenges in my life was caused by my consuming too much alcohol at one stage, and this quickly turned into a massive problem for me. Eventually I was drinking so much that I often found myself without motivation to carry on in my normal working and family life. I was drinking far more than any person could normally handle, and I think that in my mind, I came to rely upon drinking as a cure for my depression and so be able to face my life and its daily problems.

This went on for quite some time, although it never really affected my working life, nor did it change my character in any way, as I never became violent or incoherent, and most people around me had no idea of the problem I was struggling with. My wife knew, of course, and I feel very fortunate in that she stayed by me and did all she could to help me through this dark period.

But after some years of living with this problem, I decided one day that I didn't want to drink any more, and the following morning on getting up I told my wife that I was never going to drink another drop of alcohol. To begin with, it proved very difficult for me, and I visited several agencies to try to get some help. But I couldn't find the help I needed so badly and so decided to do it on my own.

Each new day was a battle to be fought alone, and even though I knew I had a serious drinking problem, I would never admit to myself that I was in fact a chronic alcoholic. But eventually, after several weeks of going without a drink, I did come to terms with the idea that I *was* an alcoholic, and I feel certain that if I hadn't stopped drinking when I did, I would not be alive today. I was also having a lot of health issues at the same time, and so it was an uphill struggle. But I am glad to say that I succeeded in that battle, and I have never taken any alcoholic drink since that time.

And again, my advice to anyone reading this book who may suffer from the same problem, or worse, perhaps that of drug addiction, is to always seek help. I managed to battle it on my own and with my wife's support, but it was a tremendous struggle, and not everyone would be capable of seeing it through. There are many associations and charities that will help, and so I repeat, seek out help, and with a little will power you will come out on top again. I am the living proof of that.

***

Moving to Northampton was certainly a change of direction for myself and my family, and we owe such a lot to the town and the people in it. It has been a wonderful experience, and after so long living here we have a great many friends and associates, while the experiences that we have gained will never leave us.

We were able to buy a house at a reasonable price with help from the government, and that too made all the difference for us at the time, as it meant no more rent for us to pay. I have continued to prosper locally, and I have achieved so much far beyond any of my expectations.

Looking back now, I wouldn't change the decision we made to move to Northampton from London, and nor would I change anything we have been through since our move here over fifty years ago now. Northampton has become my hometown, and I feel I am a true Northamptonian after living and working here, and then serving on the Town Council and as Mayor, for so many years.

CHAPTER TWENTY-THREE

My visit to Lourdes

I undertook a visit to Lourdes, in France, in 2024, which proved to be a wonderful experience for me. I was struggling with a few health problems at the time, and so I had a carer to take care of me and push me around Lourdes in a wheelchair. My walking had deteriorated quite a lot in the months leading up to the trip, and I was walking with the aid of a walking stick.

Lourdes is a large town in the French Pyrenees, and it has become a global centre of Marian pilgrimage, receiving hundreds of thousands of visitors each year. Many Catholics believe that the Virgin Mary, the mother of God, appeared 18 times at the Grotto to a young girl, St Bernadette Soubirous.

Originally a sleepy market town on the road to the spas of the Pyrenees, Lourdes has grown into the largest Marian pilgrimage centre in the world. The town has two sections: the international portion by the river, consisting of the spiritual area containing the Grotto and churches (known as the Domaine or the Sanctuaries), and the "French" portion, centred around the Marketplace & Hotel de Ville.

Pilgrims go to Lourdes with a desire to visit the Grotto where Bernadette supposedly saw the Virgin Mary. It is a place of prayer, trust, peace, respect, unity and silence that visitors can take advantage of in different ways. In front of the Grotto, on the far side of the Gave River, benches allow pilgrims to spend time in silence and meditation about everything that invades their thoughts: suffering and worries but also joys and thanks. Spiritually, in the Bible, the Rock symbolises trust in God, the stone on which the Church is built, the solid word on which we lean.

Lourdes holds a unique place in the world, as no other shrine, regardless of religion, benefits from the permanent presence of a doctor in charge of noting, verifying and investigating cases of supposed cures. Many pilgrims are seriously ill and visit Lourdes in the hope of receiving a cure, which some believe is miraculous. Over 7000 cures have been registered since such pilgrimages began, but only 70 have been recognised as miraculous by the church.

It is, of course, very much a question of personal faith and belief, but it does install a sense of wonderment in all those who have visited, even those without true faith, and there is an atmosphere always present that particularly struck me and stayed with me during my visit as a fervent catholic.

My visit was organised by my church, and a group of us were to meet and set off from the church at 3 AM. My wife drove me to the church, from where a coach would drive us to Stansted Airport. I was again suffering quite badly from depression at the time, and so was on antidepressants. I wasn't feeling too good, but it was pleasant to find our priest outside our Church. He had come to see us all off with a prayer for a safe journey.

I was allowed to sit in front of the coach, but at about halfway to Stansted we had to take an obligatory detour, and shortly after this the coach crashed into a bridge. The coach driver was in a bit of a panic, and I had to calm him down. He told us that the coach was stuck, and we all became a little anxious, thinking we might be late for our flight and so miss it. But the driver eventually managed to free the coach, and we were soon on our way again, a little behind schedule but still with time enough to reach the airport.

On arrival at the airport, we were split into two groups, and the first group went through the departure process with no problems. But when it came to the turn of the second group, of which I was part, they informed us that because of the chaos at the airport at that moment we couldn't be processed in time to board the plane before its scheduled departure time, and so they couldn't let us through to the plane under any circumstances.

I thought to myself then that we'd be returning home, but the leader of our group reassured everyone that we would get to Lourdes, no matter what. We waited nervously while enquiries were made, and we were informed that we would spend the night in a hotel at Stansted, and early the following morning a coach would drive us to Gatwick airport where we would take another flight to Lourdes. Our trip had been saved.

But on arriving at Gatwick early the following morning, we were informed that our flight wouldn't leave until 8 PM that evening! By then I was completely stressed-out by the changes in our itinerary and the constant delays, but the other people in the group were very considerate towards me and reassured me that everything would be fine. My carer, David, escorted me all through that long day of waiting in the airport, taking me around in a wheelchair, and he really was brilliant and caring throughout the whole journey.

We eventually boarded a flight that evening, which took us to Bordeaux, and from there we took another coach journey to Lourdes. When we finally arrived at our hotel in Lourdes, the group who'd managed to take a flight on the previous day were all outside to greet us, clapping and cheering as though we were intrepid heroes! I was just very relieved to have arrived at last, and anxious to get to my room and indulge in some much-needed sleep.

One day I went through a most curious experience which I will never forget. David had taken me in my wheelchair to the underground chapel in the Grotto, which was huge and very impressive. I thought about how difficult it must have been to build the chapel in that place.

David pushed me to the front and left me there, and I found myself quite alone to meditate and pray silently. Then suddenly, without warning, my wheelchair seemed to be shaking and rocking up and down, while I was invaded by a calm and warm feeling deep inside. I opened my eyes to find myself focused on the altar, in front of which the cardinals and bishops were celebrating a mass. I turned my head, thinking that it might have been David shaking my wheelchair, but there was no one at all behind me, nor even close to me. I continued to concentrate on the altar, when my wheelchair then turned completely sideways to face the archbishops and members of the congregation, as I discovered when I opened my eyes again in shock, although I was still at the same place in which David had left me. To this day I still don't know what unseen force had caused the wheelchair to shake and then move as if of its own accord.

At the end of the mass, the archbishops left the altar and came smiling in a procession past me, and they all stopped and shook me by the hand. The others in my group were very pleased to see the Cardinal and the archbishops shaking my hand. I wouldn't go so far as to claim that what happened to me on that day in Lourdes was a miracle, although since it happened I haven't needed to use a wheelchair nor even a walking stick, and my general health has greatly improved.

Saint Bernadette is now one of the saints I regularly pray to, and I do believe it was her who encouraged me to take a pilgrimage to Lourdes. I was sad to leave Lourdes, as it was one of the best spiritual experiences I've had in my life, and I am so thankful to have been there as a pilgrim.

Dennis presenting the Sacred Heart Church candle at Lourdes

Dennis at Lourdes

Lourdes

The crowd before the sacred grotto

CHAPTER TWENTY-FOUR

Abington Park and my future

Abington Park, in Northampton, is a most wonderful place to visit and it has come to mean a lot to me over the past few years. With its 117 acres, it is the oldest park in the town and has been much loved and appreciated by generations of the townsfolk over many years. It was bequeathed to the people of the town by Lady Wantage in 1897, and it sits on the site of a medieval village, with some buildings having survived for over seven centuries!

It is also home to 352 different species of trees, which is the second largest amount anywhere in England, with only Kew Gardens housing more. Just to walk around the park surrounded by so many trees and so much greenery is an uplifting experience, and it is almost like experiencing the natural lifeblood of the town.

There is a lovely ornate bandstand which hosts a variety of local brass bands and concert bands, as well as folk, jazz and pop music throughout the summer. The Park also contains two lakes and a model boating lake, connected by a stream. There are numerous species of ducks there who will happily relieve any visitor of seeds and crusts, as well as a pair of swans, and dozens of wild birds worth bringing the binoculars for, including a flock of green parakeets. A densely wooded spinney also provides some great squirrel and bird-watching opportunities.

There is a well laid-out children's playground, a large café that serves drinks, snacks and meals, tennis courts, bowling greens, outdoor table tennis, an aviary and a rose garden, as well as the mediaeval church of St Peter and St Paul. A sensory garden for the blind, open to all, is planted with numerous fragrant and pleasantly textured plants and flowers for all your stroking and sniffing pleasures! It is established in the gardens of what were once the cottages of the working farm that was part of the original village of Abington. A quiet haven for the solitary reader, or writer.

The 500-year-old Manor House, once the heart of the family life of those who lived there, is now the Abington Park Museum, a Grade I listed building. The museum is also home to the Northamptonshire Regiment and Yeomanry gallery, and it has a full and varied events and activity programme throughout the year.

The Park Café, established in 1975, is owned and run by Mr. Tony Ansell, a friend of mine who was also a Councillor, as well as Mayor of Northampton in 2018. It has become the meeting place of a group of my friends, and we meet there several times each week to share a coffee and to catch up on the latest gossip and events around the town, including football scores and generally trying to put the world to rights.

Tony Ansell, far left, owner of the Park Cafe

When my wife, Rona, was Mayoress of Northampton, she planted a Rowan tree in the park, close to the café, with a plaque recording the date and the event. We also attended a great many concerts and events in the park over our Mayoral year, and that increased my respect and love for this unique and extraordinary place that means so much to so many Northamptonians.

I now try to visit the park almost daily, and I undertake some mild exercises on the sports' equipment installed on the main pathway running down to the largest lake. I meet some of my friends there on most days, and it was also there that I met my good friend, Peter Dietrich, about three years ago now. Peter is an author and a photographer, and he wrote one of his most popular children's books, **THE TIGER IN THE PARK**, in Abington Park during the Covid lockdown. That's why he is now known as Tiger-Pete in our circle of friends.

Dennis on an exercise-bike at the park

As I mentioned in an earlier chapter, Peter became my appointed photographer during my year as Mayor, and he has left me with a vast archive of brilliant photos and video films of almost all my events, as well as a beautiful souvenir photo album which my family and I will always treasure. There is also a copy deposed in the archives at The Guildhall.

He is a talented photographer and filmmaker, and as he frequently points out, he grew up in Northampton while living opposite Abington Park in the 1950s, which became his and his siblings' playground, and that makes it a very special place for him indeed. It is also the one place in the town that hasn't changed since his childhood, and that means a lot to him. He has also produced two Park Calendars since I have known him, and they are indeed very special to anyone who frequents the park.

I think that the story of Peter's early life is also worth mentioning here, as I find it quite fascinating. Peter's father, Heinz, was born in Germany, but as a young teenager he was sent to a concentration camp for refusing to join up with the Hitler Youth movement. He was forced to join the German Artillery forces and sent to Italy, where he surrendered to the American forces and then spent the rest of the war as a prisoner of war in the USA. After the war he was returned to Europe, and was detained for some time in Northampton, at the camp for returning prisoners of war then established on the Racecourse.

Peter's mother, Margaret, a teenager at the time, used to sing at concerts staged for the prisoners at the camp, along with Des O'Connor, with whom she was at school and who had been evacuated to Northampton from London at the beginning of the war. That was how Peter's mother first met his father, and they quickly became friends and then sweethearts. Upon his release he decided to remain in Northampton, and he and Margaret were married shortly after. He established himself as a hairstylist and opened his own salon on Abington Square. It was soon immensely popular, with people queuing outside sometimes to get their hair styled. Among his clients were Des O'Connor and the footballer Kevin Keegan.

Peter's father's shop on Abington Square, early 60s

Peter's parents went on to have eight children, while Peter eventually left Northampton and England in 1975 to work and travel as a reporter/photographer, visiting many different countries and producing documentary films and reportages about his travels around the world. He has lived in 12 different countries over the past 49 years and speaks many different languages. He is also a poet and songwriter, and his 5 volumes of poetry are much appreciated by his readers. He is the author of 3 musicals and 4 children's books. I felt very fortunate when he agreed to help me edit and revise the two volumes of this autobiography, for which help I will always be more than grateful.

He also wrote a poem for me, **SOME MEN**, published in his latest volume of poetry, **AFTER THE FLOOD**. He has agreed for me to publish this poem at the end of this book as a kind of postscript.

I have also met and become friends with another local character in the park café, the actor and showman Tony Howes. He has appeared in TV programs such as Doctors, Emmerdale and Midsummer Murders, and is well known as a Dame in different pantomimes and in touring musical shows such as The Rat Pack. His one-man performance of 'A Midsummer's Night Dream' by Shakespeare is a wonder of poetical eloquence and song, and well worth attending.

Tony Howes – A Midsummer's Night Dream

Tony is known to be a flamboyant character in our park circle, proving to one and all that the world is indeed a stage for any actor, (thank you, Shakespeare!) and his comic strength is in his understanding and self-deprecation of his own flamboyance, often a source of mirth and laughter. He is also a talented and very popular children's entertainer, and he performs regularly at the park café and other localities, as well as at private children's parties. He has appeared in several TV adverts, and during my tenure as Mayor, he helped me at several of my events in Northampton, raising funds for my two charities.

Tony now has a P.A., Janis, who takes care of most of his bookings and other matters, and I have also become her friend over our time spent together at the park café. She is also well-travelled, and often tells me stories about the different countries she has visited.

We have become a closeknit group at the park café, where we meet on a regular basis, and I do enjoy the company and conversations of all my friends there, although it would be impractical to name or describe all of them here. There are quite a few people with whom I meet and talk with, and I hope I will be able to do so for some time to come. We also organise the occasional meals together at local restaurants and pubs, and other outings that keep us occupied and in touch.

It is especially pleasant in the summer months to sit outside the café and soak up the sun, surrounded by trees and lawns and playing families and dogs, and to listen to the different concerts that take place in the bandstand on Sunday afternoons, and to hold conversations with friends and strangers, while feeling how blessed I am to have such a place to sit in, especially now I have had to give up my allotment, which was also one of my peaceful havens. So, thank you, Abington Park, for being such a wonderful place for all of us.

Group meeting at the café in summer

***

I think that brings me to the end of this second volume of my autobiography. Concerning my future, I will not be seeking re-election as a Councillor in the next elections of May 2025, as I will be 83 on my next birthday, and I think it is timely for me now to relax and enjoy life as it presents itself to me. It has been a long journey of 18 years for me as a councillor, as well as Mayor for one year, and then being made an Alderman, but It has also been an exciting journey that I will never forget or regret.

I sometimes reflect on my official life in Northampton and hope that I contributed in making my elected district of Talavera better in so many ways. I would like to thank here the many people who have helped me throughout my working life and my official life at the Council. So many have been kind to me over my long life, and I dedicate this book to all those who shared the journey with me along the way.

It was my life, in the way I lived and saw it, and this is for the moment the end of my story as I grew up and gradually transformed myself from street urchin to become the Mayor of Northampton.

I also thank God for my family and my children, and for my many friends over the years, and for the life I have lived.

SOME MEN
(For Dennis Meredith)

Some men will weep when others are dying,
Some men will sleep while others are trying,
Proud men will strut and decry as mad preachers,
Wise men will smile and then grow old as teachers,
But all men must melt when face to face with true love,
Realising at last that most light falls from above.

Some men are silent while others are seeking,
Some men won't listen when others are speaking,
Firm men will flounder on the day they must choose,
Torn men divided on how to win or to lose,
But all men must discover their own path to follow,
Knowing through crude instinct when directions ring hollow.

They threatened to lock this one man up and throw away the key,
Told him to put all his cards upon their table;
They said no man in his right mind would ever claim to be free,
But he just laughed then ripped off every label;
They likened him to a weed growing in their perfect flowerbed,
He replied more like a flower in their rotting rubbish heap;
He was nothing more than an overlooked book no-one had ever read,
Then they must be empty vessels into which stagnant waters creep;
They said he was a raving fool who blindly believed in angels singing,
He replied that at each fading end we must all face our shining beginning;

Then if we lock you away right now you will be alone with your empty pages,
He smiled and told them the most beautiful birdsong is heard coming from desolate cages.

Some men develop claws while others bare grinding teeth,
Some men carry worse weapons stashed underneath,
Angry men will discard all love and then march off to war,
Gentle men will plant gardens as did the first men before,
But all men must acknowledge the inborn strength of each stigma,
Kneeling then with humility before the vast reach of Life's enigma.

Peter H. Dietrich - 2023

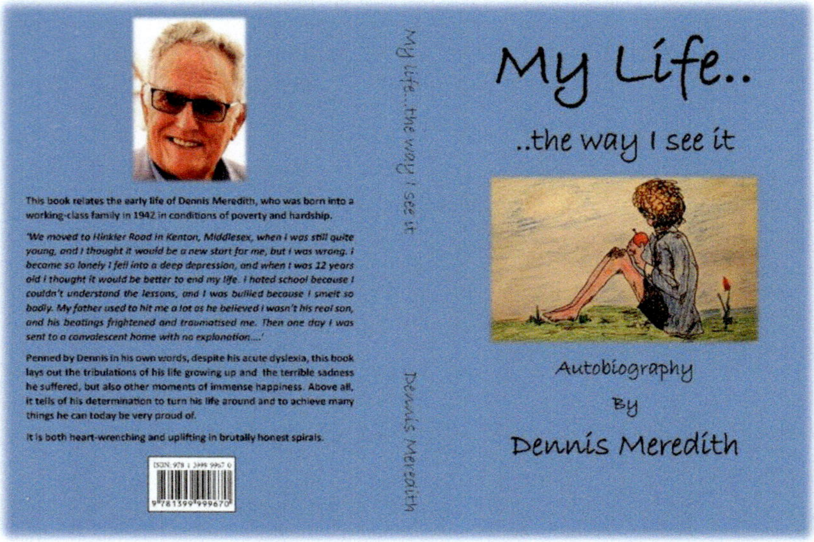

The first volume of Dennis Meredith's autobiography is also now available

----

First published in the United Kingdom – 2025

Contact: dwg4246@gmail.com